CAIRNS

CAIRNS

Messengers in Stone

David B. Williams

THE MOUNTAINEERS BOOKS

THE MOUNTAINEERS BOOKS
is the nonprofit publishing arm of The Mountaineers,
an organization founded in 1906 and dedicated to the exploration,
preservation, and enjoyment of outdoor and wilderness areas.

1001 SW Klickitat Way, Suite 201, Seattle, WA 98134

© 2012 by David B. Williams

First edition, 2012

Distributed in the United Kingdom by Cordee, www.cordee.co.uk

Manufactured in the United States of America

Copy editor: Julie Van Pelt
Cover and book design, layout, and illustrations: John Barnett/4 Eyes Design
Frontispiece: *Harri Mutilak* by John Barnett/4 Eyes Design

Library of Congress Cataloging-in-Publication Data
Williams, David B., 1965-
  Cairns : messengers in stone / by David B. Williams.
    p. cm.
  ISBN 978-1-59485-681-5 (pbk) – ISBN 978-1-59485-682-2 (ebook)
  1. Cairns. 2. Waymarks. 3. Signs and signboards. I. Title.
  GT3910.W55 2012
  659.13'42—dc23

                    2012012632

ISBN (paperback): 978-1-59485-681-5
ISBN (ebook): 978-1-59485-682-2

SUSTAINABLE
FORESTRY
INITIATIVE
Certified Chain of Custody
Promoting Sustainable Forestry
www.sfiprogram.org
SFI-01268

SFI label applies to the text stock

To my father,
who was always there with an encouraging word,
unqualified support, and enduring love.
I miss you dearly.

℘

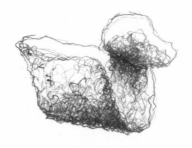

Duck cairn

CONTENTS

A classic cairn

INTRODUCTION

They seem never to have been a warlike race; passing through their country, we once observed a large stone cairn, and our guide favoured us with the following account of it: "Once upon a time, our forefathers were going to fight another tribe, and here they halted and sat down. After a long consultation, they came to the unanimous conclusion, that instead of proceeding to fight and kill their neighbours, and perhaps be killed themselves, it would be more like men to raise this heap of stones, as their protest against the wrong the other tribe had done them, which, having accomplished, they returned quietly home.

–DAVID LIVINGSTONE,
Narrative of an Expedition to the Zambesi and Its Tributaries

Once upon a time, or so the Brothers Grimm tell us, Hansel and Gretel lived near a large forest with their father and stepmother. This being a fairy tale, the evil new wife used the pretext of a great famine to convince the father to abandon his miserable little cherubs in the woods. Upon overhearing the plan, Hansel slipped out of the house and filled his pockets with white pebbles, which he dropped while hiking into the woods with his parents. He and Gretel then followed the stones back to safety.

But wickedness is persistent, so during the next famine the stepmother tried the same trick again. This time, however, she locked the door at night to prevent any enterprising youth from collecting white pebbles. The next day, the ever resourceful Hansel ripped a small hunk of bread into pieces to use as trail markers.

Unfortunately for Hansel and Gretel, the birds of the forest got to the bread before they did and ate all of Hansel's crumbs. The kids got lost without the trail markers, made the mistake of nibbling an edible house, and ended up in the clutches of another fairy-tale trope, an old witch, who thought they would make a good meal. As we all know, Hansel and Gretel escaped, finally made it back home—where their stepmother had died—and lived happily ever after.

I retell this story for one reason: to focus on Hansel and Gretel's back-country skills. Clearly they chose the wrong material for marking the trail. I am not blaming them for their poor decision. Hansel made the best of a bad situation when he scattered bread crumbs, but could he have made a better choice?

Although child psychologist Bruno Bettelheim wasn't known for his hiking prowess, in his groundbreaking *Uses of Enchantment: The Meaning and Importance of Fairy Tales*, he offers a wise observation in regard to this question. He writes that on Hansel's second trip into the forest "he did not use his intelligence as well [as on the first trip]—he, who lived close to a big forest, should have known that birds would eat the bread crumbs. Hansel might instead have studied landmarks on the way in, to find his way back out." How much happier would Hansel and Gretel have been had they paid better attention on the trail or used a better way to mark the trail?

As most hikers know, one of the best and simplest ways to mark a trail is to pile up rocks into a cairn.* Neither size nor shape really matter. An effective marker might simply be two narrow rocks placed vertically next to each other, a small pile located on one side of a trail fork, a massive pile high on a ridge and visible for miles, or a big rock with a little one on it pointing toward the correct route. This latter style might be the origin

*Throughout the book I use *rock* and *stone* interchangeably. Some writers argue that *stone* implies a human connection whereas *rock* refers to the raw material, untouched and unaltered by humans. I see their point but also think it has to do with size. *Rock* often implies large or part of the earth. Consider the biblical "Rock of one's salvation" or Shakespeare's "Alas the sea hath cast me on the rocks." No one would substitute *stone* for *rock* in these cases. *Stone*, in contrast, often refers to smaller objects. *Rock*, of course, can be used in this regard as well. Because I am generally referring to a *stone* or *rock* that can be picked up by hand, I figure that both terms sound right; therefore, my use of *rock* or *stone* has more to do with how the word sounds or how often I have used the other term.

of the term *ducks,* an equivalent to *cairn* often used in the Sierra Nevada of California.

Using cairns to mark trails occurs around the world, from far north in the Arctic south into Argentina; from the Himalayas to the shores of the seven seas; from the deserts of Arabia to the forests of the Amazon. There are the *tugong bula* of Borneo, the *alamat* of Egypt, the *milladoiro* of Galicia, the *ahu* of Hawaii, the *nana'shûñpi* of the Hopi, the *varða* of Iceland, the *tsé ninájihí* of the Navajo, the *mojoneras* of the Tarahumara, and the *isivivane* of the Zulu, to name a few.

Cairns have also served as more than just trail markers. Lost explorers have built cairns, hoping that the rocks would protect precious journals or notes. In many Native cultures, tired travelers spit on a small stone and added it to a trailside cairn as a way to transfer and eliminate fatigue. Inuit people across the Arctic erected cairns called *inuksuit* that helped drive caribou to a communal kill site. Cairns mark territorial boundaries, good hunting grounds, places of danger, burial spots of dead relatives, territories of historical significance, sites to appease a deity, and locations to seek good luck.

In each of these situations, cairns become a form of communication. When we didn't all carry cell phones or GPS units, cairns provided an enduring message from one person to another. The message didn't require any special knowledge or tools to send or receive. It could be communicated no matter the weather or season. When you saw a cairn, you knew what it meant. Now, as more people travel to new places, cairns still communicate in a timeless language. Their layered meanings may not be transparent to people who aren't local, but they still tell the visitor, you are here, you are not alone.

Ultimately, cairns have been an essential guide aiding travelers for thousands of years. As Hansel and Gretel learned, paying attention on your journey can be critical, but we don't always do so. In such a situation, nothing is more reassuring than finding a cairn, silent messenger of the trail.

Small rock cairn

I.

CAIRNS ON
THE TRAIL

I've just used cairns to get from here to there and there to here.

— JIM WHITTAKER,
first American to summit Mount Everest,
correspondence with author

I am not sure I should start a book that celebrates cairns by noting that, in addition to building cairns, I destroyed them for many years. I was even paid to do so by the federal government. Technically, cairn destruction was not in my job description, but I still did it while wearing a uniform. The uniform was the green and gray, known to some as a pickle suit, worn by National Park Service rangers. This was in the middle 1990s when I walked the trails of Arches National Park in southern Utah.

Arches is ideal cairn-making territory with unlimited rocks for stacking, wide-open and unforested terrain, and many enticing sights that draw people off the park's well-established and brilliantly conceived trail system. Some trails, such as the route up to Delicate Arch, go through areas completely devoid of vegetation. These situations required that we mark the trail with cairns, or else there would be no obvious route across the open expanses of rock. Curiously, some of the cairns on this trail consisted of only one rock. Before my years at the park, trail crews had taken sandstone blocks about the size of shoeboxes, drilled a hole through each one, and skewered them with rebar cemented into the base rock.

We did build traditional cairns on our other trails. We rangers knew that they were more than adequate to provide directions to the key features of the park. Visitors apparently disagreed, and they would add cairns along the route. I admit there were no officially designated cairns, but when I saw cairn after cairn after cairn, I knew it was time for a little cairn busting.

No official protocol existed. I would take the rocks and try and disperse them in some sort of natural way, which presented a challenge. Placing a rock so that it looked natural in a landscape festooned with rock wasn't hard. Getting the stone to that location was the challenge. If you have spent any time in southern Utah, you have encountered signs alerting you to the presence of biological soil crusts. Also known as cryptobiotic soil crusts, they are an alliance of cyanobacteria, green algae, fungi, mosses, and lichens. Cryptos, as they are lovingly called, form the dominant ground cover, functioning as a sort of nursery, stabilizing soil, increasing water infiltration, and providing nutrients to other plants.

Cryptos have a problem though. They suffer when trod upon by boot, bike, and beast. Thus the old adage of "Take only pictures, leave only footprints" does not apply in the desert Southwest. Leaving a footprint on soil crusts curtails all of their functions. They need decades to recover, with some species of mosses and lichens taking 250 years to return to full size and function. As we used to say, "Don't bust the crust." Because of this, I couldn't walk anywhere I wanted to place the offending rocks. I had to carry rocks to dry washes, hop from rock to rock, or do a delicate tiptoe through the crypto and then make sure I didn't compound the cairn problem by dropping a rock on soil crusts.

In addition to building cairns near our cairns, visitors liked to put up cairns leading from park trails to some exciting feature they had discovered. These were the cairns that caused the most wrath and scorn within the ranger world. Not only did the visitors go off-trail, leaving evidence that even Dr. Watson could have followed, but their cairns would entice others to follow, compounding ecosystem damage and occasionally causing hikers to get lost. Another ranger suspected that some people purposely took down our cairns and built their own in the hopes of leading other visitors astray.

I relished destroying these cairns. I know this can be construed as an elitist attitude. It wasn't illegal to go off-trail at the park, as long as you avoided the cryptos, so what right did I have to destroy someone else's wayfinding markers? I did it for two reasons: extraneous cairns lead to environmental degradation, and it's against the law. Federal regulations prohibit the disturbance of rock in national parks.*

I was not the lone ranger busting up cairns. For example, Charlie Jacobi has tried to rein in a decades-long infestation of cairns at Acadia National Park in Maine. "Some places looked like Easter Island," says Jacobi, the park's natural resources specialist. In 2002, he set up an experiment to see if additional information would limit cairn building on the South Ridge Trail up Cadillac Mountain.

About fifty to a hundred hikers ascend the 3.5-mile-long route every day. Beginning in a thick forest of spruce and pine, the trail soon leaves the woods and continues on open domes of granite before ending at the 1,530-foot-high summit. The trail is marked by Bates cairns, which consist of two large rocks supporting a lintel, on top of which sits a single pointer rock. The name honors Waldron Bates, who first built this style of cairn in the early 1900s.

For the initial part of Jacobi's project, crews tidied up the sixty-seven Bates cairns between the summit and a prominent trail junction. Then rangers hiked the trail every five days for the next month, recording changes to the cairns and restoring them if necessary. Visitors altered roughly a third of the cairns during each monitoring period. They most often added rocks to the Bates cairns but they also removed rocks, destroyed one cairn, and built an additional sixteen cairns.

Next, Jacobi's crews posted the following sign in three places along the trail: "Cairns are carefully placed piles of rocks built by trail crews to mark trails and guide hikers. Adding to cairns or building other cairns

---

* Chapter and verse of the *Code of Federal Regulations* section that applies to national parks reads, "Except as otherwise provided in this chapter, the following is prohibited: (1) Possessing, destroying, injuring, defacing, removing, digging, or disturbing from its natural state:...(iv) A mineral resource or cave formation or the parts thereof."

or rock objects detracts from the natural landscape, causes soil erosion and plant loss, and misleads hikers. Do not add to or build cairns or other rock objects. Leave the mountain and the rocks as you find them." Rangers again checked the cairns for the next thirty days. Cairn alteration dropped significantly, from 35 percent changed to fewer than 20 percent changed, though people destroyed three more cairns than in the previous month and built an additional fifteen of their own.

Ten years later, Jacobi sees little long-lasting effects from his experiment. "We're knocking down cairns all over the place," he told me. "The mountaintops are being dismantled. Most hikers think they are seeing a natural landscape, but everything now is in the cairns."

We have no idea how long people have been piling up stones to mark the way, but I don't think it's a stretch to say that we have been doing it forever. I know there is no way to prove this, but I would contend that we are not the lone species to build cairns. Paleoarchaeologists have indirect evidence that *Australopithecus afarensis*, the species made famous by the Lucy skeleton, used some sort of stone tool around 3.4 million years ago. In 2010, an article in *Nature* described cut marks on two bones found in Ethiopia, one from an animal the size of a goat and the other the size of a cow. Although the researchers could not locate a tool, they concluded that the bones' cuts and scrapes were deliberately made by a sharp stone.

If all Lucy did was pick up a sharp rock and slice a piece of meat for her lunch, it still takes some thought to do this, and if she could make this leap of cognition surely she could have piled up a rock or two to let her family know where she was going or where she had left that recently killed animal. (You might argue that eating is more important than finding your way, thus Lucy would think harder about solving her food issues than leaving a record of her whereabouts. But not knowing how to get back from where you went often forces some rather critical thinking.)

Moving closer to the present, paleoarchaeologists have direct evidence of stone tools from 2.5 million years ago. The tools look like hand-sized river cobbles that have been worked to give them a sharp edge. Made by *Homo habilis*, they have been found across Africa. It seems obvious to me that these earliest members of our genus must have built cairns. How else did they communicate to their kin that they were heading out to colonize new territory? Cairns, at least, would have also helped them on the return route.

In this sense, cairns can be seen as one of the earliest forms of communication. Even if you move forward in time and just focus on *Homo sapiens*, this argument has merit. The world's oldest artwork dates to around forty thousand years ago. Whether the cave drawings in France or the voluptuous Venus figurines, in each case the artist has attempted to communicate an idea, a belief, or a feeling. The artist lets others know, "I am here." It seems reasonable that such abstract thoughts of these earliest artists would have been preceded by cairns, which after all make a similar statement, with far less effort required.

A corollary to this conundrum is the question of who built that first cairn, a male or a female. We have no way of testing this question or proving an answer, but I tend to think it was some guy. Circumstantial evidence in favor of males includes that guys like to play with rocks, to build and engineer things, and to throw rocks. Not that there aren't gals out there who do all of the above, but these seem to be predominately male traits. (I wouldn't be surprised if someday researchers find that the cairn-building gene is related to the rock-throwing gene.) But how to account for another classic guy trait, not asking directions? Men are notorious for their failure to admit they don't know where they are, so why would they build or even follow cairns? Perhaps building cairns is an atavistic urge, hardwired from our earliest history before we knew how to ask for directions.

The question of which way to go is one of the central reasons that humans have mounded up rocks for thousands of years. We have done so to let others know where we were going, to enable others to follow or find their own way, and to provide information for returning. At its core, then, cairn building is an act of generosity, something you do to help others. In this interpretation, making a heap of rocks that guides another fits the definition of altruism, or doing something for someone with no expected return or reward.

We are the only altruistic species, and so ingrained is this trait that children as young as eighteen months old act for the benefit of others. In a 2006 study described in *Science*, toddlers picked up a clothespin if they recognized that the person who dropped it needed the object to achieve a goal. Otherwise, the kids ignored the clothespin. This could explain why children like to build cairns: they are practicing to be altruistic later in life. The implication is clear. Since building cairns is altruistic, and altruism is a human trait, building cairns is a profoundly human act, right up there with making art, writing, and speaking.

Being human also means that, unlike other animals, we need artificial enhancements to aid our navigation. We can't sniff our way back like a salmon, track the earth's magnetic field as monarch butterflies do, or detect polarized light, a trait that allows some birds to migrate thousands of miles. Seasoned travelers do, of course, make use of many clues to find their way—such as noting the topography, tracking the movement of the sun and stars, and observing where plants grow—but not at the level of, say, a homing pigeon.

I worry though that new technology may render our use of natural clues and cairns obsolete. More and more people now carry GPS units in the backcountry, so much so that the classic urban "hunch" of a person bent slightly, head tilted down, staring at a screen, has become a common trailside feature. Are these people relying too much on technology and not enough on the subtle details around them? Will they no longer look for that reassuring cairn letting them know that others have been there before?

The answers to these questions depend on how you use a GPS unit. The technology does provide many advantages, allowing navigation in the dark, in bad weather, off-trail, and in areas without cairns.* Using a GPS unit may also prevent you from following cairns built in the wrong location or by people for their own purposes only. The technology also comes with a positive environmental impact. If you use a GPS unit to

---

* I was once in the Needles District of Canyonlands National Park with three friends trying to find a route in the low light of a winter dusk. The lead person was looking carefully for the next cairn when he stopped. Each of us ran into the person in front, like a some classic Bugs Bunny cartoon. Not that a GPS would have helped us find our route, but it may have prevented the cliché collision.

THE JUNK AND THE SALIENT

Climbers and mountaineers often rely on cairns to point the way both up and down mountains. A well-placed cairn popping out of the mist at the top of the correct descent route down a big peak sparks the same feeling in me as a lit-up gas-station sign when my car has been running on empty for a half hour through a dark night: pure joy. That tight-gut feeling disappears, and I know salvation is at hand.

But cairns are only useful because of their nonconformance to the landscape; nature doesn't stack rocks. If there are too many cairns, then they stop being unique and stop being useful. Once a cairn loses its individual identity it becomes nothing but a pile of misleading rocks among other piles of misleading rocks. Rather than providing information and guidance, a crowd of cairns confuses the situation.

I once followed a nice set of well-linked cairns off the top of a peak in the Canadian Rockies; the route flowed well, but the ground lacked the telltale signs of travel that a popular descent route usually shows. After an hour of descending, I found a final cairn teetering near the edge of a blank cliff. There were no rappel anchors, so whomever had made the cairns had backtracked, as I now had to do. I knocked over every one of the damn misleading cairns on the slog back up. Perhaps the builder had wanted to as well but couldn't bring himself to destroy his or her hard work. Slacker.

In some popular hiking areas, the cairns are spread like darts thrown by an unskilled marksman, and I take great pride in knocking the outliers over. Cairns are the original "crowd source" communication system, but, like on the internet, not all information is good. It's up to us to parse the junk cairns from the salient ones and to edit out the junk. Plus, it's fun to knock 'em over.

WILL GADD is a rock climber, ice climber, and paraglider.

note your trail, then you don't have to build a cairn, which not only leads to less habitat destruction but also means that you don't leave any sign of your presence, a sure way to make some hikers happy.

I wonder, though, how the GPS-reliant will entice their children up the trail? Several friends have told me about how cairns kept them going during their early hiking and backcountry trips. Sometimes it was their parents using the enticement of a cairn—"When we get to the next cairn you get a treat." Sometimes it was a game to see who could find the next cairn first. And I admire the imagination and nerve of one friend's parents who told her that gnomes made the cairns and if she was very observant she might see a gnome herself.

So how do you build a cairn on a trail? You might not think that piling up a bunch of rocks requires any design knowledge or special skills, but enough issues abound that British singer and drywall expert Dave Goulder has described building cairns as a "real minefield." Height, width, location, and something called *batter* (the slope of the stone) can cause any cairn builder great despair. After all, you don't want your cairn to "look like a giant cow-pat," writes Goulder.

Location is paramount. In case you wondered, the *Appalachian Mountain Club (AMC) Field Guide to Trail Building and Maintenance* offers this practical admonition: "Cairns should be placed in conspicuous locations." Knolls are better than hollows, but a ledge or mound—that is the aspiration of any conscientious builder. Goulder suggests building near an abyss, to have a place to toss troublesome materials.

A good location requires good rocks. Large and flat ones are key for the base. What goes in the hearth or center is less important, as no one will see it, which provides the opportunity to toss in superfluous material, if you lack a nearby abyss. Refrain from collecting small rocks, as you may want to use them as wedges, a practice frowned upon by those who write instructions on how to build a cairn.

With rocks in hand you can start to build. The US Department of Agriculture's *Trail Construction and Maintenance Notebook* tells us in the section titled "Installing Reassurance Markers" to "make the base of the

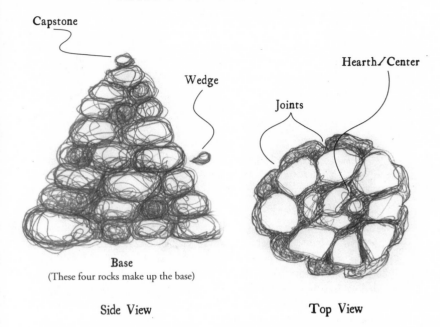

Capstone

Wedge

Hearth/Center

Joints

Base
(These four rocks make up the base)

Side View   Top View

cairn wide enough to provide enough batter for stability." Who says the government doesn't offer sage advice? A term of uncertain origin, batter refers to how a stone tilts; as the AMC guide informs us, "Each layer should...slope toward the center of the cairn." If you do this correctly, then gravity will take over and "tend to stabilize the cairn's construction."

Your work is not done yet. As the cairn rises, you must ensure that every stone has at least three points of contact, which prevents unseemly and destabilizing stone wiggle. All joints must overlap or bridge each other too. Finally comes the capstone: "Well, obviously one big stone rather that lots of wee ones," writes Goulder. If you are feeling truly altruistic, you might consider a light-colored rock as a way to make your cairn more visible.

Of course there is no right or wrong way to build a cairn. These are merely guidelines culled from a few official documents. If you want a simpler, and older, suggestion you could turn to *The Book of Woodcraft and Indian Lore*, written in 1912 by Ernest Thompson Seton, cofounder

WARNING

THIS IS THE TRAIL

TURN TO THE LEFT

TURN TO THE RIGHT

of the Boy Scouts. He wrote that "first among the trail signs that are used by Scouts, Indians, and white hunters, and most likely to be of use to the traveler, are axe blazes on tree trunks . . . but there are treeless regions where the trail must be marked."* In such a treeless situation, all you needed to do was place a small stone atop a large one. To signal a left or right, add another small stone on the side of the larger one's base. Three stacked stones meant "Important" or "Warning." "These signs . . . are used in the whole country from Maine to California," wrote Seton.

For thousands of years, and across cultures and continents, we have piled up stones to mark our way. What does this action say about us? From a practical standpoint, it means that someone or some group has desired to move between point A and point B. They may have been traveling for trade; to visit members of their family or community; to reach an agricultural area, hunting ground, or ceremonial spot; or, as we do in modern times, to seek out a specific location, such as a viewpoint.

Because we can't navigate the way many animals do, we have had to rely on our large brains to figure out how to move between two distant points. In Australia, the Aborigines created their well-known songlines,

---

* Several years ago, my wife and I were lucky enough to help build a short section of trail around Siberia's Lake Baikal, the world's oldest, deepest, and most voluminous lake. In order to show people where we would construct the trail, our leader marked the route. He didn't use ax blazes or Day-Glo survey tape. Instead, he plucked the five-inch-long leaves of an understory plant (*Bergenia crassifolia*), the leaves of which had turned scarlet in the fall weather, and placed them as markers on broken-off limbs. Siberians also make a tea from this plant, which "helps keep you young," or so one of the locals told us.

which embed the landscape in songs that allow for extensive navigation. The same sharing of directional details via song also occurs with the Inuit. In each case, the songs highlight landmarks essential for travel through a complicated landscape.

Few of us sing our way across a landscape, but we still use landmarks in our daily lives. For example, in my hometown of Seattle these include the Space Needle, Mount Rainier, and the Olympic Mountains. These landmarks are large, distinctive, and visible from many locations. And they each carry at least two meanings: The Space Needle is a reliable way for me to locate myself in the city; it is a directional aid. Mount Rainier and the Olympics, on the other hand, while providing some navigational capacity, are more landmarks for home. I feel a deep connection to Rainier. I love to see the mountain when I return from more extensive travels. It is comforting and a symbol that I am in the right place.

Cairns carry these dual senses too. We build a cairn to create a landmark that guides our travels and allows others to take the same route. Unlike my urban landmarks, of course, cairns are small-scale features, but they share the assets of having a distinctive shape—and one easy to recognize—and of being conspicuous, assuming the builders followed the wise advice of the gang at the Appalachian Mountain Club. A cairn, then, can be considered a tool, or what the *Oxford English Dictionary* defines as "a means of effecting something." As a tool, a cairn is yet another example of a defining human characteristic.

Just as when I see Mount Rainier, cairns on a trail can be reassuring too. I suspect that many of us have felt that calming effect when hiking and we come across a cairn, confirming that we are on the trail and not lost. But cairns also represent something more. I would guess that few people take rocks from a cairn and bring them home as a souvenir. If anything, people add to the pile. Each time we add a rock or build a cairn, it is a way to leave a little part of ourselves in the landscape. The cairn becomes a tangible sign of the bond between people and place, an acknowledgement of a relationship that we value. Cairns are a sign of community—of hikers, of family, of humanity.

Not bad for a little pile of rocks.

Chimney cairn

2.

THE GEOLOGY
OF CAIRNS

The old rule about the end product being the sum of its parts
certainly applies to cairns. It can only be as good as the materials
supplied, and like arches, pillars, etc., the builder is always going to
see some part that would have been tidier-looking had there been
a better choice of stone. But surely this is where the craft comes
into its own. Any builder or mason can create a fine structure using
good, flat or block stone, but to do it with a heap of dog's heads
and highwayman's hats takes REAL SKILL.

— DAVE GOULDER,
Notes on Building a Cairn

If you want to travel to the perfect location in the world to
build cairns, I recommend going to Iceland. Flying into the airport
at Keflavík, you get a glimpse of the cairn builder's paradise you are about
to enter. None of those pesky green things called trees mar the landscape.
Birches, willows, and dwarf shrubs covered much of Iceland at the time of
settlement, in 874, but logging, livestock grazing, and land clearing have
left the country with a mere pinch of its historical vegetation. This means
that wherever you build a cairn, it will stand out, visible in all directions.

Once on the ground, heading the forty miles to the capital of
Reykjavík, you will see a second reason for happiness: rock is everywhere,
a result of the little island sitting atop that giant zipper called the mid-
Atlantic ridge. For more than 150 million years, North America, Africa,
and Europe have been moving apart along this six-thousand-mile-long
crack in the earth. Also known as a spreading center, the ridge consists

of parallel mountain ranges separated by a rift valley, where the tectonic plates are spreading away from each other in opposite directions. Out of the rift has spilled the floor of the Atlantic Ocean—black, oozy, slow-flowing lava that cools to hard basalt.* The only place the mid-Atlantic ridge appears on land is in Iceland, which has led to widespread and regular volcanism, a fantastic source of rock for cairns.

Cairn builders can further rejoice because Iceland is forming above what geologists call a mantle plume, or hot spot—basically a huge, deeply buried Bunsen burner that melts rock, which then rises toward the surface. Other hot spots include Hawaii and Yellowstone, both areas rife with volcanic activity. In Iceland, this double dose of magma generators translates to a volcano erupting about every three years.

One nifty aspect of all of this active lava spewing is that when you build a cairn in Iceland you are building with some of the youngest rocks on earth. Geologists are regularly criticized, or at least misunderstood, for their reliance on what writer John McPhee called Deep Time—the millions and billions of years of earth history. You don't need to worry about Deep Time in Iceland; on the Westman Island of Heimaey, for example, just thirty minutes south by ferry from the mainland, you can build a cairn with rock born in 1973. Plus, the stone is a beautiful brick red, which makes for a most handsome cairn.

Young rocks have another splendid trait. Unlike older rocks that have been smoothed and degraded by the agents of erosion, Iceland's freshly made basalt has an uneven, rough surface that is competent and hard. A typical chunk of Icelandic basalt has distinct edges and well-defined corners that link together well, in contrast to the rounded shapes of rock worn down by ice and water.

Cairn builders gain even more from the physical characteristics of basalt. Because it forms on the surface, as opposed to deep underground in a chamber, basalt cools relatively quickly, particularly in the upper layers of a lava flow. Rapid cooling gives basalt the texture of an airy sponge cake, with abundant cavities and a jagged, irregular surface. These

---

* The rift and mountain ranges look like what happens when you run your fingers through sand—a narrow trough, or valley, bordered by ridges. The lava erupts out of the valley and cools to form the ridges.

textures result in blocks of basalt that latch together in a Velcro-like manner and make cairn construction easy and satisfying.

Cairns are everywhere in Iceland. On one trip, I found small stacks and immense piles, single cairns marking twisted trails through lava flows and dozens next to prominent viewpoints. At one spot alongside the country's main road known as Laufskalarvarða (Laufskalar's Cairn), hundreds of cairns commemorate a farm destroyed in 894 by the eruption of the Katla volcano, less than twenty miles to the east. Tradition holds that adding a new stone to the farm site brings good luck. But even in a land of rampant volcanism, rock can run out, so the Icelandic Roads Administration trucks in rocks for people to use.

My favorite Icelandic cairns, though, stand in the broad, flat valley of Þingvellir. Here, around 930, the early settlers of Iceland gathered to hold the Alþingi, or general assembly. It was the world's first parliament, an event held annually until 1798. More exciting to my little geologic mind, though, was seeing the exposed mid-Atlantic ridge where the North American and Eurasian tectonic plates are spreading apart.

We arrived on a sunny, very windy, and cool day. After a quick stop at the visitor center, we descended a wide gravel path. On our left a lichen-encrusted wall of basalt rose straight up. To our right the layers of basalt tilted into the valley. After climbing over a couple of the walls and crossing a narrow creek, we found a trail over and through the broken-up flows of basalt. Still in late winter, leaves had not popped out on the birch and willows, but a spongy, inches-thick carpet of moss blanketed the basalt and gave it a frosty hue of green and gray.

Cairns dotted the length of the trail, which ran for about three miles. All of the cairns were modest, about three- to four-feet tall, and all were made of basalt boulders, speckled with orange, gray, and black lichens. The cairns weren't really necessary, as the path through the moss was distinct, but I still found them reassuring and downright satisfying—they were made of rock from one of the world's most unusual geologic spots, one of the few places on earth where the great tectonic plate boundaries are at the surface, and the one place where a cairned trail leads on a walk from North America to Europe.

At the most basic level, building a cairn doesn't involve much thought. Gather some rocks and put them in a pile. But there is a problem. Not all rock is created equal. Some, such as Iceland's basalt, is ideal stacking material, but other rock, such as shale—soft and easily fractured—tends to resist piling into a long-lasting cairn.

If you do plan to build a cairn, chances are high that you will work with sedimentary rock, such as sandstone, limestone, and shale, which covers about 70 percent of the earth's land surface. These rock types come in a variety of colors, textures, and strengths, but all share a common origin: they form from the deposition of sediments, either bits of other rocks, precipitated minerals, or organic matter.

Sedimentary rock is normally deposited in horizontal sheets, also known as layers or beds, which can range in thickness from fractions of an inch to many feet. Bedding is usually an asset for cairn builders because the bedding plane between two layers is a zone of weakness. When the stone breaks along bedding planes, it often has two flat surfaces, always a handy feature when fashioning a well-made heap of stone.

Sandstone, and its various cousins—including shale, mudstone, siltstone, and conglomerate—form from the breakdown of other rocks. Wind, water, and ice pick up the detritus and ferry it into lakes, seas, deltas, alluvial fans, and deserts. Once deposited in layers and buried by additional material, the sediments slowly compact, as the weight above forces out water. Subsequently, groundwater carries in cement, which fills the pore spaces and binds everything together into rock. A sediment that has undergone this process is said to be lithified, or literally turned to rock.

The lithification of limestone—a rock primarily made of calcium carbonate, usually in the form of the mineral calcite—takes a different route. Calcite can precipitate chemically directly out of the water and settle to the bottom, like spices in Italian salad dressing; or it can come from bones and shells, which can lead to rocks rich in fossils. Limestone generally forms in lakes and seas but can also form in hot springs, such as at Mammoth Hot Springs in Yellowstone National Park. This rock is known as travertine and, while not a common component of cairns, has long been used as a building stone, most famously in the Colosseum in Rome.*

Generally a splendid building material, limestone in some locales can present a pointed challenge for cairn builders. The beds of rock are so hard and sharp that sitting on or holding the blocks is treacherous. (In college, we dubbed this *tearpants limestone*.) If you don't want to apply tush to stone, you may not linger near it—and you will miss the opportunity to build a cairn with a rock that resists erosion, weathers slowly, and has distinct edges.

If you happen to be in an area devoid of sedimentary rocks, then more than likely you will have to build a cairn of igneous rock. Forged in the bowels of old Vulcan's smithy, as described in a nineteenth-century Iowa newspaper, these are the rocks that get the headlines, that shut down air travel, and that star in movies best branded as disaster porn. Igneous rocks originate from the cooling and crystallization of molten rock, also known as magma, when it's below ground, and lava when above.

Igneous rocks come in two basic varieties: those that solidified within the earth and those that hardened on the surface. The underground type—known as intrusive, or plutonic, rocks—solidify slowly, which typically generates relatively large minerals (visible to the eye) in a fine-grained matrix. Extrusive, or volcanic, rocks cool on the surface and crystallize so quickly that they tend to be fine-grained and not have visible minerals.

Granite is the best-known and most common plutonic rock. Basalt wears the same crown for the volcanic clan. Other igneous rocks include pumice, obsidian, diorite, and andesite. The names depend on the minerals found within the rocks and whether the rocks formed on the surface or underground. Nearly all have qualities well suited to cairn building.**

---

* Without fossils, distinguishing between a chemically and a physically deposited sedimentary rock can be difficult. The easiest way to determine one from the other is to put a drop of dilute hydrochloric acid on a fresh surface. Limestone fizzes and sandstone does not. If the limestone is very compact-grained, meaning it is made of very small particles, limestone blocks sometimes have a slightly musical tone when you rap them with your knuckles.

** The one that doesn't is pumice, which is so rich in gas pockets that it floats. Pumice is sort of equivalent to the foam (light and gassy) that shoots out of soda pop when you shake a can. Curiously, after Krakatau erupted in 1883 people discovered great rafts of pumice that floated for years and traveled thousands of miles, which lends credence to my fantasy of building floating cairns.

Like basalt, most break with jagged edges, distinct corners, and rough surfaces. They are generally very hard and less prone to erosion. And, because the major US mountain ranges—such as New Hampshire's White Mountains, the Sierra Nevada, the Cascades of Washington and Oregon, and many parts of the Rockies—consist primarily of igneous rocks, this type of rock is widespread and abundant in areas where you might want to find or build a cairn.

The granite of the Sierra Nevada possesses one more characteristic that aids cairn constructors. During the hundred million years since it crystallized deep underground, uplift by plate-tectonic action and erosion of the overlying rock have combined to lower the pressure on the granite, allowing the rock near the surface to expand and crack as if a massive girdle were removed. Because these expansion cracks run parallel to the exposed surface, the weakened stone breaks off in sheets and slabs, like layers of an onion, providing acres upon acres of rocks for cairns.

Metamorphic rocks make up the third node of the geologist's rock-classification scheme. Least common on the surface of the earth, they include two of the most distinctive, or at least most recognized, rocks: slate and marble. Consider these two rocks the most utilitarian and the most prestigious stones, respectively. Slate has been used for refrigerator shelving, urinals, electrical panels, roofing, pool tables, and of course blackboards. Marble, in contrast, has a more rarified pedigree. The Greeks built the Parthenon from it; Michelangelo sculpted with it; and corporations cover their walls with it. Marble is shorthand for "We can afford the very best."

Formation by pressure and temperature unite metamorphic rocks. Metamorphism is a complex process based on a simple idea of converting one rock into another without melting the original material. Small-scale, or contact, metamorphism occurs when magma gets injected into pre-existing rock and bakes it. Metamorphism also takes place when rocks pile atop other rocks. A good example is the marble of Carrara, Italy, which started out as limestone deposited two hundred million years ago.

There it sat until about twenty-seven million years ago, when a small tectonic plate plowed into Italy. Acting like a bulldozer, the plate pushed thousands of feet of rock into a mountain range atop the limestone. Deep underground, temperatures rose to between 570 and 850 degrees Fahrenheit and converted the underlying limestone to marble.

No matter how they form, metamorphic rocks don't go through a molten phase. What changes is their texture, structure, and mineralogy. Such changes almost always generate the same type of rock from a preexisting source. For example, a cooked shale becomes slate, metamorphosed granite can become either schist or gneiss, and a baked and squeezed sandstone becomes quartzite.

Regarding cairn builders, the critical element of metamorphism is that high pressure reorients minerals within a rock. In an unmetamorphosed rock, minerals generally lie catawampus to each other, with their main axes pointing in every direction. When compressed during metamorphism, however, the minerals begin to rotate and align, like a deck of cards. The aligned minerals act like a bedding plane, facilitating the splitting of rock into layers, a feature that led to the names of three metamorphic rocks: Slate comes from the French *esclater*, "to split"; phyllite from the Greek *phyllon*, for "leaf"; and schist from the Greek *schistos*, "to split," as also in schism.

The property of easily splitting into sheets should make a stone such as slate an ideal cairn-building material but typically doesn't. Slate splits too easily, resulting in very thin layers, as shown by its use for roof tiles and blackboards. You can build attractive and intricate cairns with slate, which has its own merits—as in the slate cairns of artist Andy Goldsworthy—but if size is your goal, you may not want to devote the time required to erect a stack with blackboard-thin slabs.

You could, however, take a different approach with slate and assemble a cairn with upright pieces. One way would be to lean them against each other to form a pyramid. Or you could erect a single slab, held in place at the base, creating a sentinel or finger-like cairn. Such cairns stand at Castle Crag in England's Lake District, where they look especially mystical in the gray mists of the mountains.

Rock type isn't the only geologic factor that dictates cairn construction. A second factor is the mantra of real estate agents—location, location, location. Cairns built in the desert will age differently than those built alongside a river or in the mountains. Precipitation, temperature, plant life, and proximity to water all affect the weathering rates, and hence the shape of the rocks, not only before you might use them, but also after they have entered that higher state of entropy known as a cairn.

Consider two possible materials for building a cairn: At one extreme you might use bowling balls and at the other, fruitcakes. With little

CAIRNS AND ENVIRONMENTAL IMPACT

It might be safe to say that the largest and grandest cairn in all of North America is New Hampshire's Mount Washington. Loftiest summit in the White Mountains, 6,288-foot Washington is also the highest peak in America east of the Mississippi River and north of the Carolinas. A northern latitude, a couple of ice ages, and a hundred million years-plus of erosion have given this mountain a harsh façade. Its upper reaches and summit consist primarily of alpine tundra and broken talus, making it one giant rock heap.

Crusty locals, long weary of the onslaught of hikers (most of whom hail from urban centers to the south, primarily Greater Boston), entertain thoughts of deconstructing the mountain. If every visitor to Mount Washington could just take one rock home with them, they fantasize, soon New England's highest summit would be gone—and so too would all of that summer traffic and commotion, restoring tranquility to New Hampshire's northern reaches.

But the region's economy would go too, as Mount Washington attracts millions of tourists, who bring millions of dollars to the Granite State. In the summer of 1986, when I was a young forestry student at the New Hampshire Technical College in Berlin, I landed a summer dream job—backcountry effort you could fashion a pillar of fruitcakes. But no matter your skill with bowling balls, you could never make a pillar with them; you would always end up with a conical structure with a low angle of repose, or the maximum slope at which a pile of loose material is stable.

You would face a similar range of shapes if working with rock. At the bowling-ball end of the extreme would be river cobbles. As rocks roll in the water, they knock off each other's corners, over time fashioning a rounded shape. After the rock has settled in the stream, a continuous flow of water further erodes away any extraneous points and leaves behind a

ranger in the White Mountain National Forest. Among my duties: help all of those Mount Washington visitors by providing them with better trails.

It was during that summer, with help from fellow Forest Service workers and the Appalachian Mountain Club, that I got to build a trail on Mount Washington itself. We spent a week in the hazy August sun extending the Nelson Crag Trail two-thirds of a mile over Ball Crag to connect with the Alpine Garden Trail. And while trail building usually entails pulaskis, shovels, saws, hoes, and rakes, this job just required backbreaking rock hauling. No tread work. No trenching. No water bars. Just constructing a series of cairns several feet high and placed close enough to be followed in a thick fog (a common occurrence on Washington's summit).

But building a trail primarily by lining up cairns, simple as it seemed, still required an environmental impact statement. It was important that none of the rocks we moved disrupted Mount Washington's rare and endemic alpine plants. In essence, our rock building was meant to keep people walking on rocks and not onto the rare vegetation-harboring tundra on New England's biggest rock pile!

CRAIG ROMANO is the author of eight guidebooks on hiking and exploring Washington State (not Mount Washington).

polished surface without any edges. A similar effect occurs at a beach as pounding waves pummel rocks and round and polish them.

Any cairn built of water-beaten rocks will have a relatively low angle of repose because the rounded rocks will slide past each other. Their lack of roughness can't counter the pull of gravity. This is particularly true of hard igneous and metamorphic rocks, which can take a high polish. To build a cairn with steeper sides, use larger rocks and/or rocks of different size, both of which can increase the amount of friction between rocks and make the pile more stable. And, as the clever folks at the Appalachian Mountain Club counseled, tilting the rocks toward the center makes them less apt to slip out of the cairn.

No amount of judicious mixing of large and small cobbles, however, will get you around one of the basic facts of water-rounded rocks: the only shape you can build with them is a pyramid. Because they lack flat sides, sharp edges, and distinct corners, you can't use rounded rocks to make a stable vertical stack or, say, one with an hourglass shape. You can incorporate them into such cairns, but ultimately beach and river cobbles limit what a cairn will look like. To get creative, you need to go to the fruitcake end of the extreme.

A layered rock, such as a sandstone, exemplifies this shape. In the deserts of Utah and Arizona, where a lack of rain and plant life translates to reduced weathering rates, rocks retain their sharp sides and corners. During more than two decades of hiking desert trails, I saw many places where people had stacked sandstone blocks into cairns that resembled chimneys. Although these columnar cairns may look more stable than a pyramid of cobbles, that is not necessarily so: both shapes, by definition, are at an equilibrium at their angle of repose.

Take one of those cairns made of planar stones up to the tundra or the alpine zone, however, and it may not fare as well. When the temperature is above freezing, water penetrates into the layers of each sandstone block. Keep the temperature above freezing, and little change happens. But if the water turns to ice, it expands about 9 percent. Over geologic time, repeated freeze/thaw cycles slowly pry apart the layers, ultimately reducing a cairn to rubble.

Salt can wreak havoc on stone too. Cairns built along a beach suffer when salt in the air lands on them and infiltrates the rocks' pores. As the salt crystallizes, it expands and weakens the rock. Some forms of air pollution can also lead to salt formation. For example, sulfur from a coal-producing plant in England mixed with magnesium in the building stone of a nearby cathedral built in the fourteenth century and produced salts that severely degraded the structure.

Weathering of stone does have an upside, as it allows us to determine the age of a cairn. Cairns builders rarely sign and date their work, so we must turn to chemical evidence. As stone breaks down chemically, it produces a thin rind of different-colored material. You can see this clearly on basalt, as the oxides in it mix with air and water to form an orange coat of what is basically rust. The mineral pyrite, or fool's gold, also rusts, often generating reddish streaks that make the rock look as if it's weeping. On granite weathering leads to a whitish chalk coating. Unfortunately, these rinds do not form at a set rate, and once they are more than a millimeter or so thick, they merely indicate a very old cairn.

You can also look at how the rock has broken apart to pick up clues to the cairn's antiquity. How granular is the surface?* Do harder features, such as fossils or veins of minerals, stand out? None of these are truly diagnostic of great age, but they do provide insights that the rocks of the cairn have been exposed to weathering for many years. Of course, you might assume that the rock was that way when the cairn builder used it, but you can probably imagine that that builder would pick unweathered rocks, rocks that he or she suspected would be around for a long time.

Cold-weather environments can enhance cairn construction too, as each spring the ground spits up rocks. Throughout New England, the apparent capacity of the land to give birth annually to new stone on cleared lands provided much of the material for the thousands of miles of stone walls that snake through the region, as well as for numerous stone piles.

---

* When my wife and I lived in Boston, I once went up to the oldest building on the Harvard campus and was able to generate a small pile of sand in just a few seconds by rubbing the sandstone blocks at the building's base. The rock, known as brownstone, had been weakened over time by regular freezing. (And just to be clear, I do regret my role as an agent of erosion.)

In alpine and tundra environments, upfreezing or frost heaving, as geologists call it, can be an important source of material for cairns by generating fields of rocks ripe for use.

During winter, as the temperature drops, soil freezes—first on the surface and then down into the ground. When the frozen layer of soil penetrates down to the top of an underground stone, a bond forms that pulls the stone up slightly and leaves a slim gap under the stone. Soil thaws in reverse, from the bottom up; and because the upper part of the stone is still locked in place, the now loose, underlying soil can fill in the void. When the entire stone is unfrozen, it can't drop back down to its original position. In essence, the stone has been pulled up toward the surface.

All factors being equal, larger stones tend to rise faster, in some places up to twelve inches in a single season. Frost heaving can even thrust stones up through asphalt. It can also tilt rocks up on end, or at least at an acute angle, as variations in soil composition and texture force up one end of a boulder more than the other end. Depending on the rock and the environment, frost-tilted slabs can look finger-like, as if pointing the way for hikers.

The effects of frost heaving and other natural processes of weathering have a secondary effect on the world of cairns. In some cases, upthrust rocks can resemble cairns, stacked piles of rock, boulders propped up by another stone or stones, boulders split in half, or simply a peculiar-looking stone that looks unnatural. (Turtle-shaped rocks or piles seem to have a special appeal to those who see animal shapes in natural heaps of stone.) Such oddball rocks have attracted great attention and have led to the belief that many of these natural collections of boulders are man-made.* They have been described as mounds made by Native Americans, as sites for astronomical observance, and as evidence of Celts from Ireland visiting America more than three thousand years ago.

* Piles of stone that look like people built them are visible in the Brooks Range of Alaska. In a 1972 article in *Arctic and Alpine Research*, geologist Warren Yeend described rock piles that "one could readily imagine . . . had been deposited by a larger dump truck." He concluded that these piles had formed from rocks being dislodged by frost wedging and then rolling or sliding down steep chutes and out a snowfield onto the valley below, where they piled up in a hole or ice ridge. Such piles, called protalus mounds, could accumulate up to 1,000 feet from their source.

I don't doubt that some of these rock piles do have a human origin, but as Robert Thorson, author of one of my favorite books on geology and people, *Stone by Stone: The Magnificent History in New England's Stone Walls*, told me, "If you see ten thousand stones, it is always the odd one that will get attention. Sure, some will look like a turtle, but that doesn't mean every rock is a man-made turtle." Thorson compares this belief in the human origin of natural features to the belief in Bigfoot. Despite scientific evidence, people don't want the real answer; they want the fiction, he says.

I agree with Thorson that some people are seeing exactly what they want to see. I also think that humans often try to understand what we see, and the simplest explanation is to relate what we see to what we know. Most of us know little about rocks and geologic processes, whereas we like to think that we know a lot about humans—or at least we can relate to people more easily than we can to rocks, so it makes more sense to give rocks a human origin rather than a natural one.

Maybe that is one of the appeals of cairns, that someone has taken a bunch of rocks and humanized them by placing them in a pile. We intuitively sense that a cairn represents a cross between the realm of geology and the realm of humans. Both realms are rich, and when they intersect—whether in the form of an earthquake, a volcano, or a cairn—it merits our attention, draws us in, and gives us a richer connection to the world around us.

Beinakerling

3 ·

THE ECOLOGY
OF CAIRNS

Into every empty corner, into all forgotten things and nooks,
Nature struggles to pour life.

— HENRY BESTON,
The Outermost House: A Year of Life on the Great Beach of Cape Cod

If you have ever doubted the long-term effects that a few people can
have, consider the case of those who lived more than four thousand
years ago in the holy lands of the Middle East—in particular, those who
dwelt in the hills now known as the Golan Heights. Rising above the Sea
of Galilee on Israel's eastern border, the once-forested lands were home to
shepherds and farmers. These Bronze Age people lived in thatched-roof
houses made from the local basalt. For food, they tended sheep, donkeys,
and goats, which, in addition to providing sustenance, generated a compact fuel source, suitable for burning. They also grew wheat, peas, and
lentils and harvested acorns and olives.

When someone died, the survivors built elaborate tombs consisting
of two or more vertical basalt slabs, called orthostats, holding up a single
larger flat stone. These massive roof stones could easily weigh several tons.
The tombs ranged from fairly simple structures—just three slabs erected
on the ground surface or slightly below—to massive tombs that included
several roof stones and orthostats, with courses of smaller boulders providing additional structure. The biggest tombs, or dolmens, as archaeologists

call them, could be seventy-five feet long.* They were cut into the ground and covered by a heap of dirt and stones called a tumulus.

In the 1970s, ecologist Didi Kaplan noticed a botanical enigma in the Golan Heights. Archaeological research showed that a tree known as the Tabor oak had grown in widespread forests that had covered the Golan hills in the Bronze Age. Now only isolated oaks remained, "puny reminders of erstwhile woodland," as archaeologist Clare Epstein put it. The dearth of trees wasn't the enigmatic part; centuries of harvesting had removed the oaks. What intrigued Kaplan was the distribution of the living oaks in the area where he worked, the Yehudiya Forest Nature Preserve. Most of the 15- to 20-foot-tall oaks grew out of the mounds of stones that remained from the tumuli and dolmens erected thousands of years ago. Commonly referred to as cairns, the rock piles ranged in size from 13 to 26 feet wide and 3 to 9 feet tall. All consisted of gray basalt boulders. When Kaplan later studied the trees in the late 1990s, he discovered a direct connection between the microhabitat of the cairns and the oaks.

Tabor oaks grow widely across Israel and even merit a mention in the Bible. Right after the prophet Samuel anoints Saul as the first king of Israel, he tells the new king to go to the oak of Tabor, where he will meet three men who will give him bread. Despite their apparent importance to prophets and kings, Tabor oaks face a tough life. If the acorns aren't buried or protected by duff, they dry out and die. If the seedlings don't get enough water in the arid landscape, they die. If animals graze the seedlings and saplings, the plants die or become more susceptible to fire and increased herbivory. If no grazing occurs, grasses can proliferate, which allows rodents that eat acorns to thrive.

Kaplan found that the cairns left over from the dolmens and tumuli shelter the oaks from their natural hazards. For instance, two species of mice collect acorns, some of which they eat but some of which they cache in the protective habitat of the cairns. Within the boulder mounds, the acorns obtain additional moisture because they face less competition

---

* The word *dolmen* was first employed by the French archaeologist Théophile Malo Corret de la Tour d'Auvergne and is said to originate in Breton, derived from *tôlven*, or "table stone," but more likely from the Cornish *cromlech*, or "hole of stone."

from grasses, which don't grow in the cairns but flourish in the surrounding area. The cairns also protect the soil under the rocks, which acts as a sponge, accumulating and storing moisture, in contrast to unshaded areas where the soil rapidly dries out. Finally, the ancient stone piles protect seedlings and saplings from fire and grazing. Because of this microhabitat, more than 90 percent of the mature Yehudiya Preserve Tabor oak trees grow within the confines of the cairns.

Kaplan's study also shows that adult trees prevent younger ones from thriving within a cairn. They do so by selfishly sucking up the available moisture. But when that adult dies, younger oaks eking out an existence within the confines of the rock pile have their chance and shoot up, trying to take over the cairn. From deaths thousands of years ago to the more recently departed, there is rebirth and renewal in the cairns of the Golan Heights. Perhaps this is what resurrection in the Holy Land is all about.

As Kaplan observed, from an ecological point of view a pile of rocks can be more than just a pile of rocks. Because cairns form a three-dimensional space above a two-dimensional surface, they create habitat with niches for plants and animals to utilize. The additional elevation provides perches for birds and mammals. The nooks and crannies offer lizards and snakes safety from predators. Even hikers take advantage of cairns, to hunker on the lee side out of the wind. Environmental conditions can vary enough so that a cairn can serve as an oasis.

My favorite example of how a cairn can become a refuge comes from a trek in late-August 1957 across the Libyan desert to Chad. With temperatures hitting 120 degrees Fahrenheit, ornithologist Brian Booth and others entered what he described as "one vast featureless gravel sheet . . . devoid of all vegetation, either living or dead . . . its utter barrenness is complete." Then they came across a few slabs of sandstone fashioned into a cairn for a camel trail between the towns of Kufra and Agedabia. Two sooty falcons flew out from under the cairn. As the birds circled, Booth discovered three eggs on the bare sand under one of the slabs. He didn't record the ground temperature in the sun, which probably soared above 120 degrees, but it was only 108 degrees in the shade. Booth speculated

BEHIND EVERY CAIRN...

I woke up a few hours after we'd landed the Antonov biplanes on Prince Patrick Island in Canada's far North. The eternal light of the Arctic lowers the need for sleep and the island called out for at least a small amount of exploration on our stopover on the way towards the North Pole. I set out up the nearest hill for a towering cairn, after checking to see if there had been any polar bears spotted recently. The hulking station mechanic said with a laugh, "Haven't seen no bears lately. But they are out there, mostly on the ice. When they get you, you mostly don't see them anyway, heh heh. Or you can't say whether you saw them afterwards."

This didn't sound too serious and the little I knew about bears, I figured they would stay close to the ice and the seals. The hike up the hill, the snow crisp below, the sky an envelope of blue, was a welcome relief from the confines of the plane. A pile of rocks eight feet tall rose from the top of the hill, a landmark the Eskimos used for navigation, particularly when out on the ice and the featureless roll of the land ashore all looked much the same.

that the cairn was a refuge for the falcons to rear their young at the height of the autumn bird migration, allowing the raptors to hunt their migratory prey that flew across the desert.

More often birds use cairns as perching sites. Many species, including snowy owls, ptarmigans, ravens, and prairie falcons, are known to land on the tops of cairns. They may rest, preen themselves, stand and scan the terrain, or dine. For example, I was hiking in eastern Washington across a low treeless ridge and stopped at the highest spot, a mound of basalt boulders. The cairn rose only a few feet above the ridgeline, but it

Suddenly as I approached within a few feet of the cairn, I detected a flash of movement, of fur, from behind it. I leapt back. The cairn was right in front of me, only a few feet away. There was no reason to run; I'd be caught immediately. There was still no roar, no furry paw snaking around the rocks to snap my neck. No big teeth appeared. It couldn't be too big a polar bear. The cairn was tall but only a few feet around.

It was silent; the Arctic is so silent the air hums.

There was a little scuffling noise. It was moving. All my hair prickled. A very large curved ear appeared, then another, then a black twitching nose and some big buckteeth. It was a large, complacent Arctic hare. It was so unconcerned I could have petted it. The hare stepped forward around the cairn and into the sun, and after a cursory glance at me, settled back on its haunches and went back to dozing.

ROBERT MADS ANDERSON is the author of *Seven Summits Solo* and *Antonovs Over the Arctic: Flying to the North Pole in Russian Biplanes*, and his story here is adapted from the latter.

provided a favorite spot for birds to land, as shown by the white droppings that covered the highest boulder. Around the sides I found several gray hair-laden pellets, each filled with what I guessed to be rodent bones. A bird had not only dined, it had then tossed up the undigested parts of the meal, a typical practice of owls and raptors.

When birds consistently perch on a cairn, their depositional habits can also have a quite cheery effect on the landscape. Bird droppings add nitrogen, phosphorus, and calcium and raise the pH of acidic substrates. Several species of lichen make use of these nutrients to grow bigger and faster. Lichenologists refer to such species as *ornithocoprophilous,* an outstanding word that means "bird-dung loving."

Two of the best studied of these poopophiles are *Xanthoria parietina* and *Xanthoria elegans,* known as the maritime sunburst lichen and elegant sunburst lichen, respectively. The names come from their resplendent yellow and orange coloring. For hikers, *X. elegans* is the one we most often encounter on cairns at higher elevations and higher latitudes. When you see this sunny patch of color on a cairn, you can feel confident that some bird, or some mammal, such as a marmot or pika, spent some quality time high above its surroundings.

Of course other primary urges may fire the old neural network of cairn sitters. Strong flying insects, such as butterflies, horseflies, hoverflies, and lady beetles, home in instinctively on conspicuous, isolated, optical markers and use them as waiting stations. Some will actively defend their territories, while others will merely sit and wait on a cairn till an opportunity floats by and then will fly out for a little six-legged sex. Such bug bars can attract hundreds to thousands of individuals and may not be suitable for small children.

Along with influencing where animals poop and mate, cairns also have a very localized effect, acting as a haven. As I noted earlier, hikers often make the most of the three-dimensional structure of a cairn to escape the wind. Plants also capitalize on this phenomenon, particularly above tree line, where a cairn may be the only feature around that blocks or slows down the wind.

Wind is a critical factor at higher elevations. In addition to carrying sediments that can abrade plants, wind also desiccates plants, sucking out water. When the wind travels around a cairn, it slows down, dropping litter (such as leaves and petals), seeds, snow, and soil, creating a little nursery of extra nutrients and water. For example, at Mount St. Helens, in the zone in front of the crater, which was completely barren after the volcano's 1980 eruption, plants, such as ferns and huckleberry, have colonized the habitat provided by the cairns that mark a trail around the mountain.

The wind shelter offered by a cairn can also enable the growth of one of my favorite alpine communities. Trees that grow high on mountain slopes look like they have suffered at the hands of pruners gone over to the dark side, the stunted and gnarled trees sporting a flat top. Known as krummholz, meaning "crooked wood" or "elfin wood" in German, such plants often start in the protected nook of an obstruction. Several alpine ecologists I corresponded with thought that a cairn could provide a suitable site, though boulders are more typical. Age and size were the key factors, with a cairn having to persist for at least several decades to create the necessary growing conditions.

The additional snow that accumulates on a cairn's lee side has a secondary effect. It acts as an insulator, protecting plants from the temperature extremes caused by solar gain and nighttime heat loss. A study in the Arctic by Matthew Sturm and his colleagues found that snow attenuated weekly winter air temperatures by about 40 percent and daily fluctuations by about 80 percent. Snow could insulate so effectively that it prevented soil from freezing. Not that snow is all pure and good. It can crush plants and in summer can lower soil temperatures, but it also may help facilitate plants trying to get established in the protected oasis created by a cairn.

Other plants and animals take advantage of another property of cairns, the south-facing side. By acting as a radiator, the cairn melts snow more quickly on its south side, which provides additional moisture. Plants also grow bigger and faster from the warmer microclimate generated by the cairn reflecting heat. You have probably noticed this thermal effect at home when plants shoot up next to a wall and grow more slowly just a foot or two farther away.

Cairns increase water availability in a third way. As the air cools at night, condensation forms water droplets that accumulate on the surface of rocks. Some animals take advantage of this by licking the water. (In the Namib Desert of southern Africa, an important water source for black-backed jackals comes from water condensing out of a coastal fog onto the surface of rocks.) Other animals and plants benefit from this water source because some of the water will drip off the surface to the ground below. Moisture can accumulate under a cairn as well, providing additional water for the roots of nearby plants.

In all of these circumstances, cairns are not a deciding factor in the survival of the ecosystem, but they do provide an advantage for at least some plants and animals that might not have thrived without that pile of stones.

Far away from the alpine environment, cairns in desert ecosystems create habitat used by animals. Being able to find a suitable microhabitat is critical for ectotherms, whose metabolic rate and body temperature relate directly to their environment. As ecologists Daniel Beck and Randy Jennings wrote, "Retreat to a refugia is arguably the most common and important way that small desert animals persist in harsh and variable environments." Such refugia are usually natural cracks and crevices or underground burrows, but researchers have also found various animals— from lizards to arachnids to snakes—holed up in a cairn.

By their very nature as a somewhat random pile of stones, cairns provide diverse spaces, both in the sun and in the shade. This thermal mosaic allows an animal to precisely control its body temperature simply by moving just inches between hot and cool. Furthermore, escaping off the ground surface a few inches means finding much cooler temperatures, a critical factor in the summer. At night, a good-sized cairn with larger rocks reverses the thermal situation and acts as a warming oven, slowly releasing heat as air temperatures drop.

During my years of living in the desert I can't count the number of times I saw lizards on or in cairns, even ones that consisted of just a few rocks. Often I would see a lizard out in the open and then watch it dart into the safety of a cairn. More often, the lizard was out catching a few rays on the cairn and as I approached would move back under cover.

Occasionally I would come across a lizard doing push-ups on top of the cairn. These memorable encounters were with collared lizards in their garish skin of turquoise green, yellow, and white spots and yellow feet and head. At up to fourteen inches long, these bold beasts are one of the desert's most beautiful animals. They would remain atop the cairn, flaunting their colors with a steady up/down, up/down. I was always amazed at how close I could approach these kings of the cairn.

Lizards usually do push-ups as a sign of territoriality, and a good-sized cairn may enhance a despot's reign. In a study of side-blotched lizards, one of the more common and widely distributed southwestern desert reptiles, ecologists Ryan Calsbeek and Barry Sinervo found a significant response to improving a lizard's territory through the addition of features conducive to thermoregulation. Most noteworthy was that for a dominant male, the despot, an enhanced habitat reduced the amount of space he had to defend, and he thus became less susceptible to predation. The male's progeny also profited from areas of better thermoregulatory habitat with higher growth rates and survivorship. Although they were not studying cairns specifically, Calsbeek told me that he hypothesized that if a cairn was big enough, on the order of twenty-five to thirty rocks, it could provide similar benefits.

All of these wonderful ecological aspects of cairns does not mean that you should rush out now and go build a cairn to better the lives of desert and alpine beasts. Researchers in Australia have found that when people move rocks they can have a negative impact on reptiles. In particular, Jonathan Webb and Rick Shine of the University of Sydney have spent many years studying the broad-headed snake and have found that removal of loose surface rocks has contributed to driving down the snakes' numbers to the point that it is listed as endangered in New South Wales.

Broad-heads hide out for much of the day under rocks or in crevices. As with cairns, these retreats allow the nocturnal snakes to achieve a thermal optimum. Velvet geckos, the main food source of broad-heads, have similar habits. Shine and Webb's work shows that people who take rocks away from the natural setting cause harm in part because they operate on the Goldilocks principle, choosing stones neither too big nor too thin, which robs the snakes of their ideal thermoregulating stones.

Even when people aren't taking the stones home but are using them to make cairns, they may degrade habitat. Removing stones can disturb lichens and mosses, which have grown in protected spots that provide water and sunshine. Vascular plants face similar challenges, often congregating around a water source at the edge of a rock or cairn. And, as I noted earlier, walking off-trail to get that special rock for a cairn can damage biological soil crusts and fragile alpine plants. As to their use by animals, undisturbed rocks fit the landscape like a jigsaw puzzle and form protected crevices that keep out predators and debris and keep in moisture. Few cairns achieve such intricacy. Webb told me that he supposed that "many species of reptiles defend territories; hence, if you remove twenty rocks to build one cairn, you might create sub-standard habitat for one reptile, but the remaining nineteen reptiles will be homeless." One of his PhD students discovered what happens to many of the reptiles when humans remove their rocks—predatory birds eat them.

Sometimes the clues to understanding the microhabitat effects of building a cairn require intrepid sleuthing. I learned this when reading naturalist Christopher Mitchell's wonderful little book called *Lake District Natural History Walks* devoted to the Lake District of England. Subtitled *Case Notes of a Nature Detective*, it includes eighteen walks focused on details that allow a reader to penetrate beneath the surface and to learn deeper stories about natural and cultural history.

Walk number eight winds around a small lake called Devoke Water. Mitchell begins on a grassy knoll that rolls gently down toward the lake. From what he has read, Mitchell knows that he should soon pass by a Bronze Age cairnfield, an area teeming with cairns made more than three thousand years ago by people clearing land for agriculture. But he finds none of the 160 piles of stone reported in the literature. All he sees are tufts of grass. As he looks more closely, he realizes that discreet patches of a pale-yellow matgrass dot the dark-brown fields. At this moment Mitchell has an epiphany: the matgrass is growing atop buried cairns. The hidden piles of stone had changed the drainage and mineral make-up of the soil, creating a favorable habitat for the tufted matgrass.

Continuing on, Mitchell writes that an extensive forest had covered this region up to the middle Bronze Age, when the inhabitants started to cut down the trees. They also cleared stones from fields where they planned to grow crops. During the clearing, they would occasionally toss the stones into piles at the base and sides of trees. When archaeologists in the nineteenth century came across these piles of stone, they thought they were collapsed Bronze Age structures called beehive huts. As the name implies, such huts were shaped like a beehive, round with a conical top, which over time had caved in and left behind a mound with a central hollow.

Mitchell cites work done in the 1980s by archaeologist Tom Clare, however, which showed the true nature of the cairns. Because the piles lacked careful construction, he concluded that they were evidence of Bronze Age field clearing. Eventually the trees had rotted and left behind a sort of crater, or hollow, in the center of the cairn. Clare wrote that "we might, therefore, see the mounds…as fossilising a line of vanished trees."

Each time we build a cairn it has an effect on the local ecosystem. Sometimes those effects may be felt immediately. Others times they may take hundreds or thousands of years. No matter the time involved, in building a cairn you are establishing a connection to a place and becoming a part of that community.

Bates cairn

4·

AGE DATING
A CAIRN

It must be admitted that archaeological data have an inert quality,
a certain spinelessness when unaccompanied by a more or less
definite chronological background.

— ALFRED TOZZER,
"Chronological Aspects of American Archaeology"

On August 12, 1875, Captain George Nares anchored his ship
to an iceberg on the eastern edge of Baffin Island. He planned to
place three thousand rations on Washington Irving Island, a dab of land
less than a mile off Baffin's coast and sixty miles west of the northwest
edge of Greenland. The supplies would be an emergency cache in event
of "a compulsory retreat" from Nares's goal of reaching the North Pole.
But large ice floes that could have damaged his ships thwarted Nares's
plans, so he sent food and supplies north two miles to a protected bay.
Nares then took a crew of men to climb nearly one thousand feet to
the top of Washington Irving. He wanted a better view of the ice-filled
waters, which he hoped would eventually take his ships north to what
some called the Open Polar Sea, a hypothesized body of ice-free water
that would facilitate easy passage to the pole.

On the summit plateau he found a good vista, but no view of an open
waterway, and two mysterious cairns, each about the height of a man.
Judging from the luxurious growth of lichen, Nares wrote in his account of
the journey that they were "far too old to have been erected by Dr. Hayes,

the only traveler known to have visited the neighborhood." Hayes had traveled this way twice, in 1854 and 1861. Nares searched the cairns but could locate no records of who built them.

A physician traveling with Nares also wrote about the peculiar piles of stone. The aptly named Dr. Moss noted that lichen, the vivid orange variety *Xanthoria elegans*, was so thick that it cemented together the stones of the cairns. Like Nares, Moss pondered the cairns' origin. "Who was the builder?" he wrote. "Not Eskimo. Structure and site forbade the suggestion… Perhaps some baffled wanderer, whose fate is unknown to fame… There is plenty of room for conjecture." If only Nares and Moss had had a way to determine when the cairns were erected, they might have been able to address Moss's conundrum.

An answer was right in front of them. Lichens offer a relatively easy and accurate way to age date a cairn. When someone builds a cairn, they disturb the rocks' surfaces and inadvertently kill many lichens by changing their original orientation. New lichens then begin to grow and, in essence, start a clock ticking, which if read carefully can provide a date when the cairn was built.

One of the marvels of the natural world, lichens are neither plant nor animal. They have been described as more like an ecosystem than an individual organism. They grow through a symbiotic relationship between fungi and algae or cyanobacteria, the latter two of which can photosynthesize and produce sugars and other carbohydrates. In a lichen, fungi feed off the nutrients produced by the photosynthesizers. Lichenologists call this controlled parasitism. We call it farming.

Approximately fourteen thousand lichen species grow worldwide, from the deserts to the temperate rain forests. They can live for several thousand years, even in the extremely harsh conditions of the perennially frozen Arctic. Often growing less than 0.04 inch per year, lichens put to shame the common stand-ins for slowness—slugs, glaciers, and fingernails.

Lichens come primarily in three varieties. Most common are flattened crustose lichens, so tightly attached to their substrate that they can't be pried up without destroying them. Foliose lichens look a bit more lettuce-like, with a leafy body that protrudes beyond the substrate. Fructose lichens are the most dimensional, growing as shrubby, branching bodies or dangling in long strands.*

Using lichens to date objects began in the 1950s, when Austrian scientist and avid mountaineer Roland Beschel noticed that the farther he got from the snout of a glacier in the Alps, the larger and more abundant were the lichens that grew on downstream, and hence older glacial deposits (or moraines). Closer to home, he observed a similar phenomenon on tombstones: the older ones had bigger lichens. Because he had a good date for determining when the lichens began to grow, he realized he could assemble a growth curve such that if he measured the size of a lichen, he could plot the dimensions on a graph and ascertain its age. It was a very handy tool but was initially unused in North America because Beschel wrote in German.

Finally, in 1961, Beschel published an article in English on what he called lichenometry. It prompted a free-for-all, with scientists scurrying about measuring lichen after lichen. In particular, excited glaciologists rushed out to test Beschel's work and to establish the ages of their favorite glacial features. Others followed and adopted lichenometry to measure earthquake-recurrence intervals, rockfalls, debris-flow frequency, and the age of archaeological features.

In the half century that lichenologists have focused on age dating, they have zeroed in on one genus, *Rhizocarpon*, for its widespread growth and longevity. (Several species exist but no one can identify them in the field, so most take the easy route out and simply call them *R. geographicum*.) Yellow to yellow green and usually with black fruiting patches, *R. geographicum*, or map lichen, is handsome, unusual, and noticeable. I guarantee that if you have spent much time hiking in alpine environments you have seen, or at least stepped on, map lichen.

Because lichens lack true roots, stems, or leaves, lichenologists date lichens by measuring their entire body, a structure know as a thallus.

---

* The various forms of lichens have long enamored people, including that ubernaturalist Henry David Thoreau. He once described a stream of sand as resembling "the lacinated, lobed, and imbricated thalluses of some lichen." Said flow patterns also reminded him of leopards' paws and excrement of all kinds. Oh, Henry.

They then employ two methods for determining age. In the simplest they measure the maximum diameter of the largest thallus and see where it sits on a *Rhizocarpon* growth curve. Depending on climate and micro-climate, the growth rates can vary widely, but all have the same general shape. During the initial twenty to one hundred years of what is known as a lichen's "great period," *Rhizocarpon* explode out at 0.6 to 2 inches per century. They then settle into a more mature, and much longer-lasting, period of steady growth, on the order of an eighth of an inch per century.

Once you have a size and an accurate growth curve, plotting age is very simple, although there is a problem. Using the maximum-diameter method assumes that whatever you are dating was a blank slate, that no lichen survived whatever disturbed the substrate, be it a glacial moraine or cairn.

Method two, which addresses this issue, suffers from what one lichen lover calls "mind-numbing days" of data collection. Instead of measuring just a handful of very large lichens, the lucky lichenologist, or I suspect some graduate student, measures about a thousand lichens. She then plots the size and frequency of size on a graph and determines slope. If there are older and thus larger lichens, there will be so few that they don't skew the data set. Combining this data with a growth curve provides a means to assign a date, with accurate results stretching back four thousand to five thousand years.

Archaeologist Steve Cassells of Laramie Community College in Wyoming has used the size-frequency technique to date cairns in Rocky Mountain National Park. "This is the only method that works because it assumes that not all of the lichens are killed," he says. Cassells studied five cairns built above tree line as part of a row of man-made towers, or game drives, that directed bison, deer, and elk to locations where they could be hunted. After measuring several thousand thalli, he determined that the cairns were built between 810 and 900. "Of course, they could be much older. The stones could have been added to over the years, and the dates reflect only the most recent activity, but the lichen dates still provide a point of context," Cassells told me.

In addition to Cassells's observation, lichenometric dating of cairns has two further challenges. First is that a structure as small as a cairn may not contain enough individual lichen for the "mind-numbing" data collecting necessary to form a statistical approach. Second is that, as noted in the previous chapter, cairns create a microhabitat. In an alpine environment, wind blasting on the upwind side can remove lichens, and snowdrifts on the downwind side can cover the lower part of the cairn and damage or reduce the growth of lichens.

Those who want to use lichens to date cairns face one additional challenge. *Rhizocarpon* does not grow on calcite-rich stone, such as limestone or marble. Other lichens do grow on such rocks, including the orange *Xanthoria* lichen seen by Dr. Moss. But they don't grow at easily measured rates, which has led lichenologists, glaciologists, and archaeologists to rely on additional dating techniques when investigating their particular pile of stones.

Probably the best known method of determining age is radiometric dating, specifically carbon dating. As with lichenometry, carbon dating works on a simple principle: when something dies, it starts a clock that can be read. That clock comes in the form of a rare variety of the common element carbon, called carbon^{14}. C^{14} is an isotope of carbon, meaning it has the same number of protons and a different number of neutrons, in this case two additional ones, compared to the "regular" carbon, carbon^{12}.

These extra neutrons make C^{14} unstable, or radioactive, which leads to it breaking apart, or decaying to its more stable form, C^{12}. Known as the half-life, the decay rate of C^{14} is 5,730 years. This means that every 5,730 years the quantity of C^{14} drops in half. For example, if you start with 1,000 atoms and wait 5,730 years, only 500 atoms will remain. Wait the same time again and just 250 C^{14} atoms will be left.

Although C^{14} decays, plants constantly absorb more of it so that the ratio of C^{14} to C^{12} remains constant through a plant's life. When a plant dies, it can no longer take in C^{14} so to age date an object, all you have to do is determine the ratio of C^{14} to C^{12} in the nonliving sample and compare it to the known ratio in living organisms. Because C^{14} decays relatively quickly, it only works for dating objects less than about forty-five thousand years old. Older than that and too little C^{14} remains for measurement. To date older events and items, archaeologists and geologists rely on other radioactive elements such as uranium and rubidium, which provide accurate dates back to more than four billion years ago.

Carbon dating revolutionized many branches of science, allowing researchers to apply an absolute date to everything from bone to wood to coprolites (fossilized poop). Alas, cairnologists have not benefited as much as others have; cairns by definition are made of stone, a material sorely lacking in organic carbon. Occasionally, however, a cairn incorporates organic matter. Archaeologists have used shells and charcoal buried under cairns, wood posts protruding from cairns, and peat that has accumulated in a cairn's interstices to obtain dates. All of these dates carry the caveat that the dated organic material may not have been associated with the original erection of the cairn.

Fortunately for fans of cairns, two new techniques are promising, as neither relies on living, or formerly living, organisms. The methods share a similar basis for success: When people build cairns they move rocks, which alters the orientation of the stone and the soil where the cairns used to be. The two techniques employ a rather Sherlock Holmes–like concept, observing the minutest signs of change and deducing the story of what happened.

The first method relies on a feature that attracts the attention of many a desert visitor: the black to bluish-black patina that coats many rock surfaces. Known as rock varnish, it develops from the accumulation and cementation of iron and manganese-rich dust. What visitors may not notice is that, underground, two additional patinas grow on rock surfaces: a whitish, corn flake–like coating called pedogenic carbonate and an orange layer referred to as an iron skin. These coatings range in thickness from about 5 to 600 microns—equivalent to a quarter of a dust mite's poop, up to the thickness of a credit card.

In 2005, a team led by Niccole Villa Cerveny, an archaeologist at Mesa Community College in Arizona, decided to study these patinas and see if they could determine when cairns and associated rock rings were built in the Mojave Desert of California. Cerveny's team surmised that moving the boulders for the cairns had started two clocks ticking on the development of three new patinas. Black varnish had started to re-form on the iron skin now exposed aboveground; carbonate had grown anew on the buried rock varnish; and new black varnish had developed on old black varnish that had remained above the soil. Cerveny told me that she calls this suite of coatings a catena.*

One clock was set by the new carbonate that formed underground. Because the skin incorporated carbon from roots in the soil, it contained C^{14} absorbed by the aboveground plants, which enabled Cerveny to radiocarbon date a boulder that had been flipped over to build one of the cairns. This clock provided a minimum age for the rock structure of 4,110 years before the present. Her team read the second clock by analyzing the individual layers of the rock varnish using a method called varnish microlaminations (VML).

Over the past decade or so, Ronald Dorn of Arizona State University and Tanzhuo Liu and Wallace Broecker of Columbia University have examined thousands of microscopic layers of rock varnish. They have discovered that they form in a specific and geographically widespread pattern that depends on climate. Rock varnish layers are like tree rings, proxies for wetter versus dryer periods. VML researchers have established a chart, correlating specific layers with specific time periods, so that if you can match sequences of layers you can obtain a date for when the varnish formed.

Cerveny's team used VML on a cairn where boulder movement had rotated the orange iron skin to the surface, which led to the formation of new black rock varnish on top of the orange layer. They found that the boulder had been rotated sometime between 14,000 and 11,000 years before the present.

As with the previous methods described, Cerveny's dating can be inexact. It works best in low-moisture environments, such as deserts. Otherwise, water washes away the dusts that form patinas and carries the carbonates out of the soil.

---

* You can sort of create similar patinas at home by letting an orange sit out and start to mold. After it has done this for a while, rotate it and watch as the new layers grow atop the old ones.

I now turn finally to what may be an ideal method for age dating cairns. Though we normally only hear about radiation during a nuclear disaster, radiation constantly bathes the planet, either from an external source (via cosmic rays) or from underground (through the radioactive decay of elements such as uranium). When natural radiation strikes minerals, it releases electrons, which can become trapped and stored within the mineral's crystal structure. If some subsequent event, such as building a cairn, brings that mineral to the surface, sunlight acts as a stimulus and releases the trapped particles in the form of light energy, or luminescence. Known as bleaching or zeroing, this process resets the radioactive clock in the mineral.

LIFT HERE

The Maze District is the hardest region to reach in Canyonlands National Park. To access it by the river requires floating for at least sixty miles. To access it by bike or motor vehicle requires negotiating an ugly four-wheel-drive road. To access it by foot requires a minimum hike of fifteen miles. Once you're in the convoluted landscape of red and white banded rocks, there is unlimited exploring, often in areas seldom visited by anyone, or so you think. —DBW

A friend and I once climbed up on to a butte in the Maze. It was the kind of place that no one had been to; there was not a footprint anywhere on the top. The butte was nothing to speak of. It seemed like the kind of place no one would even want to go up. So we sat down to eat, thinking we were lunching where no one had lunched before. That's when we saw, right in front of us, a little cairn. And next to it was a perfectly squared-off slab of rock with a beautifully chiseled-in word: "lift."

Age dating using optically stimulated luminescence, or OSL as it's commonly known, relies on this property to determine when some natural or artificial process buried grains of sand. In particular, OSL dating measures the amount of luminescence held within crystals of quartz and feldspar, the two most abundant minerals on the surface of the planet.

Imagine building a cairn. You pick up a rock and sand grains cling to it. As you set the rock down on your growing pile, some of those grains fall to the ground. Sunlight hits them and releases all of the luminescence out of the quartz and feldspar. The clock is set to zero. As you

Of course, we were not only surprised to find this cairn but also totally amazed to find a little cover to a secret compartment. We were sure that a spring-loaded jack-in-the-box snake was going to leap out at us, so we gingerly moved the lid with a stick. But the only thing inside was a jar with a note that said, "I hope you enjoyed finding this." At first we thought the jar was some kind of geocache, but the note also added, "If you have a good time finding this, email me." It was signed Captain Sky Pilot with an email address.

Being a park ranger, my friend ranted that this was trash, and so after knocking over the cairn he packed out the jar. Later that evening, after we had gotten home, he called me to say that I had been a party to the illegal transportation of drugs—because as he went to throw the jar away, he had noticed that it contained a joint.

GLEN LATHROP lives in Moab, Utah.

continue to build your cairn, you place a rock on those bleached grains. Out of the sunlight, radiated electrons immediately, albeit very slowly, begin to fill defects within the crystalline structure of the quartz. You have now started the clock ticking, its energy fed by a continual bombardment of radiation.

University of Washington archaeologist James Feathers has used OSL dating on projects worldwide. In 1998, he studied quartz grains from a cave in South Africa to examine human artifacts dated at 60,000 to 70,000 years old. A 2010 study in Brazil confirmed the dates of what may be the oldest human remains found in the New World. Closer to home he began a study in 2006 to determine when people built game drives (lines of cairns or upright rocks), tipi rings, and medicine wheels in the Great Plains and Rocky Mountains.

When Feathers collects sand grains in the field, he has one overriding concern: keep them in the dark to prevent bleaching. The easiest way to do this is to erect an opaque tent over the cairn, remove the bottom rocks, and drive a two-inch-wide by twelve-inch-long clear plastic tube straight down into the sediment. After extracting the tube, he wraps it in black plastic and duct tape. He illuminates his work in the tent with a red light, which does not affect the stored electrons.

Back in a red-light-lit lab, in a room protected by two black cloths over the door, Feathers and his assistants cut the tube into five sections and sort out the quartz and feldspar. They want grains ranging in size from 150 to 212 microns, or about as wide as two human hairs. These get mounted, a hundred at a time, on a quarter-inch-wide plastic disc. A laser beam passed over each crystal stimulates and releases the trapped luminescence, which can then be measured to determine a date for when someone moved a boulder to build a cairn.

Feathers told me that the big advantage of OSL dating over other forms is that it is more specific to the precise event of cairn building. Lichenometry depends on environmental factors, which are not always knowable and may not date the actual placement of the cairn. Radiocarbon dating may be even less precise because it relies on artifacts and "the strength of association," which can't always be confirmed.

Ultimately, everyone I talked to agreed that our ability to date cairns is getting better and better. No single method is perfect, but, combined, the various dating techniques can help put cairns in a chronological and archaeological context. Accurate age dating of cairns allows a comparison of building techniques, helps in understanding how people responded to climate change in the past, and provides insights into how people spread across the globe.

Good dates also make cairns that much more interesting. I don't think anyone can deny that if you were told that a particular cairn was, say, 1,200 years old, you would be more impressed than if it was only 100 years old.

So when were those mysterious Washington Irving Island cairns built? Apparently still pondering the answer to this question, George Nares returned the following summer in September 1876. He could find nothing new so he simply redated a message he had left the previous year. Five years later, the US Lady Franklin Bay Expedition, under command of Adolphus Washington Greely, stopped by the island. They found the record left by Nares. Two years passed, and again Greeley visited the cairn. No new news.*

Periodic visitors continued to stop by the cairn site over the next century. They added notes, removed notes, and speculated on the origin of what Nares had discovered. Not until 1995 did two archaeologists have the chance to conduct a thorough study of the Washington Irving cairn site.

Karen McCullough and Peter Schledermann of the University of Calgary's Arctic Institute of North America spent two days on the island. They found a large cross made of nylon strips, a rusted tin they suspected had contained Nares's 1875 note, and broken glass. Boulders north of the cross appeared to be the site of one of the original cairns studied by Nares, but the pile of stones contained no evidence of who built it or when.

McCullough and Schledermann offered what at first might sound like an extraordinary conclusion as to who built the cairns. They doubted that Inuit were responsible as "the construction of stone cairns on top of

---

* Within a year, all but six of Greeley's twenty-four men were dead, of starvation and cannibalism, at a camp sixty miles south.

prominent capes or islands was not something on which those familiar with the land would have wasted time." Instead, they looked to the east, to Norway and Norse sailors. As evidence they cited discoveries of a figurine, cloth, barrels, and iron knives left by the Norse just fifty-five miles southeast of Washington Irving Island. Radiocarbon dating placed their origin in the late twelfth and early thirteenth centuries.

They also looked for what would have been a definitive sign, a written record. In 1824, an Inuit named Pelimut found three cairns on Kingittorsuaq Island,* 530 miles south of Washington Irving on the west coast of Greenland. Inside one was a piece of basalt about the size of a Hershey's bar. Scratched lines that vaguely looked like an alphabet covered one side. They turned out to be an ancient Norse runic text, which read "Erling Sighvatsson and Bjarni Thordarson and Eindridi Oddsson on the Saturday before the minor Rogation Day [April 25] erected these cairns and cleared…" Archaeologists have dated the rune stone from between 1250 and 1350, possibly as specific as 1333.**

If only Erling and his friends had traveled a little farther north, then we might have concrete proof of who built those Washington Irving cairns. If only Nares and his men hadn't destroyed them. Fortunately, we are showing greater respect for cairns. Fortunately, we are now developing tools to answer one of the essential questions of cairnology.

---

* Sometimes spelled Kingigtorssuaq.

** In 1968, Alf Mongé, a US Army–trained code breaker, proposed that a thirteenth-century Norwegian runemaster, Oirvar Valrslethn, had hidden a secret message on the stone by incorporating the first "poly-alphabetic substitution cipher system with variants" ever used. According to Mongé, Valrslethn had written the rune in 1244 and had actually completed his thoughts, adding "a way through the ice" to the end of the text. Apparently he did so for the "amusement of like-minded colleagues," wrote Mongé. Few others believe in this interpretation.

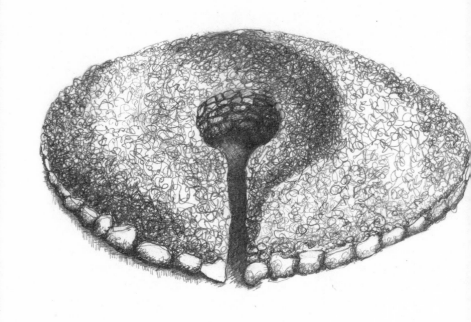

Cairn, Balnuaran of Clava

5.

BURIAL CAIRNS FROM THE BRONZE AGE

The oldest visible structures in the Scottish landscape, as indeed in many parts of western Europe, are the immensely ancient burial places built by the earliest farming communities in our land. These structures were built of stone and covered by a cairn. . . . After knowledge of their original purpose had been lost, they were still perceived as mysterious and awesome.

— AUDREY HENSHALL AND GRAHAM RITCHIE,
The Chambered Cairns of the Central Highlands

T hat venerable well of word wisdom, the *Oxford English Dictionary*, states that the word *cairn* originated in sixteenth-century lowland Scotland. Derived from the Gaelic *carn*, cairn refers to a "heap of stones." The earliest known use of it comes from poet William Stewart, who in 1535 penned *The Buik of the Croniclis of Scotland*, a poetic translation of a history previously written by Hector Boece. Stewart wrote, "Syne sumptuslie vpone his graif they set, Ane carne of stonis together cumulat, Rycht round and rownid vpone a rycht huge hycht, That mycht be sene in euerie mannis sicht." "Stones piled high for every man to see" —certainly a description that most modern people would understand.

Cairn occurs in all of the Celtic languages, including Old Irish and Welsh, the latter of which has two definitions for the word. The feminine *carn* refers to the aforementioned heap, whereas the masculine form indicates a hoof or a haft of a knife. This latter sense apparently designates a pile of stones atop a mountain, visually equivalent to a horn on a head.

A Scottish man or woman may also call a single man-made cairn, a *prop*, a term that originated in the fifteenth century and that can mean any marker used by a person, such as a stick in the ground. Just south of Scotland, in the English county of Cumbria, the locals have yet another word for a summit cairn or other prominent point of a mountain: *man*, as in the high point known as Coniston Old Man. They have also been known to call a cairn, a *raise*, a term derived from the Old Norse *hreysi*, for "heap of stones."*

The Scottish ecologist Adam Watson told me that cairn also refers to a stony patch on a hillside, as well as a stony hill, as in his beloved Cairngorm Mountains, an area he has studied for eight decades. Cairngorm is an anglicization of the Gaelic *An Carn Gorm*, "the blue hill." Historically, the name of the range was *Am Mondah Ruadh*, or "the red hill range." Though one might suspect color-blind cartographers for the name change, the newer name came into prominence in the late 1700s when English travelers visited the area and stopped in a town with a good view of the range and the specific mountain Cairn Gorm. Locals prefer the nickname Gorms, says Watson.

The British further make use of the word cairn in a way not found in the United States, nor much in any other part of the world: they use cairn as an archaeological term for a "deliberately constructed pile of stones or stone rubble, often forming a burial mound or barrow." In this sense, cairn usually refers to burial chambers, or tombs, constructed out of large slabs of stone—megaliths—and covered in boulders.** Because the cairns come in different shapes, archaeologists have developed a litany of modifiers—including ring, tor, stalled, heel, horned, and long—and all types contain one or more chambers. There are also regional styles such as the Clava Cairns near Inverness, the Maes Howe Cairns of the Orkney Islands, and the Orkney-Cromarty Cairns, also found on the islands just north of the Scottish mainland.

---

* One such raise, the Dunmail Raise, sits in the middle of a road in the Lake District. Legend holds that it is the burial place of Dunmail, the last King of Cumbria, who died in 975. William Wordsworth commemorated him in verse: "that pile of stones/heaped over brave King Dunmail's bones/His who had once supreme command/Last king of rocky Cumberland."

** Here *cairn* is similar to *dolmen*, a term preferred by the French.

TO MARK A SPACE

A year after my father and stepmother were killed by a grizzly bear along the Hulahula River in Alaska's Arctic, I traveled the same river to find their final campground. I brought communion from my priest in Seattle. I knelt and prayed.

And then I stood up, slowly, and paced the midsection of the beach where Dad and Kathy would have pitched their tent. The river had risen and fallen again since their trip. The sand was firm at the far edge by the willows. It amazed me that a river could wash away a cataclysm in a year. My eye was drawn, then, to a rock that was partly buried in the sand and out of place on a sandy beach. I looked around and saw another, and another. Five rocks, evenly spaced in a pentagon shape. This was where their tent had been, rocks securing the corners on the sandy beach against the wind. This was the place they died. Violence had been done here. Life had been lost here.

The wilderness ethic is to leave no trace. But it seemed something should mark this *thin place*, as the Celts called it, this place where the boundaries between worlds were especially light. I pried up each of the rocks in the pentagon, sand wedging under my fingernails, and carried them to a spot above the high-water line, just under the copse of willows where their bodies had been found. I pulled other rocks from the bottom of the river. The icy water cooled me through my dry suit while sweat ran down my back from the hot sun.

Finally there were rocks enough for a small cairn. I looked at it, unsatisfied. I found two small pieces of driftwood and secured a cross with a piece of twine. Then I took the tiny amulet from Our Lady of Guadalupe blessed by Father Jack in Healy and laid it on the cairn, letting it slip down in the dark space between the rocks. I stepped back, slowly, and the energy drained from my body. "I love you," I whispered to the cairn. I heard the wind moving over the tundra and out to the sea.

SHANNON HUFFMAN POLSON is a writer who lives in Seattle with her family and spends as much time as possible in her home state of Alaska. This piece comes from a memoir she is writing.

Locals favor more colorful names. Cubbie Roo's Burden on the Orkney island of Rousay is a cairn traditionally held to be a pile of stones dropped by the giant Cubbie Roo while on his way to build a bridge. Also in the Orkney Islands but now gone was my favorite named cairn, the Wart of Kirbister. Twenty miles north of Inverness is King's Head Cairn, long held to be the final resting place of the severed head of a king and the bodies, and heads, of those who died with him. The nearby Clochan Gorach translates as "foolish stones," said to refer to impious rabble-rousers turned to stone for dancing on the Sabbath. Carn na Croiche points to a worse fate: it means Cairn of the Gallows, in reference to human bones from a seventeenth-century execution.

More than 450 cairns in Scotland have been described, with more known to have existed and conceivably an equal number destroyed with no evidence left behind, according to Audrey Henshall, the authority on the cairns of Scotland. For more than five thousand years, the stone piles have been integral features on the rolling hills, moors, and bottomlands of Scotland's mainland and islands. The cairns have astounded and perplexed people, with some claiming that supernatural beings constructed them, whereas others have attributed the structures to Druids, Romans, or Scandinavian pirates.

Not all, however, were impressed with the stone monuments. When the linguist Samuel Johnson and his biographer James Boswell visited the cairns near Inverness on August 30, 1773, Boswell recorded that "Dr. Johnson justly observed that, 'to go and see one druidical temple is only to see that it is nothing, for there is neither art nor power in it, and seeing one is quite enough.'"

No one knows who built Scotland's first cairn or when they did it. Scottish archaeologists agree, however, that the cairns resulted from a fundamental change in the lifestyle of those living around 4000 BCE. Prior to this time, in what is called the Mesolithic, or middle Stone Age, a hunting and gathering lifestyle predominated. Seeking out available plants and animals, the people moved seasonally to exploit the natural resources. As archaeologist Colin Richards notes in *Vessels for the*

Ancestor, "physical *movement* [italics his] from place to place define[d] life and, therefore cosmology."

With hunting and gathering slowly giving way over hundreds of years to agricultural lifestyles in the early fourth millennium BCE—in what archaeologists call the Neolithic—new ideas began to take hold. Planting crops and tending domesticated animals led to a less mobile life. People no longer had to travel seasonally for their livelihood; they could remain in place and thus develop a connection and commitment to what now could be called home.

Having a home place also brought a new emphasis on death. As people established a long-term attachment to place, they began to perceive a continuity between those who came before and those who now worked the land. They began to watch as time passed, as the human-generated cycle of planting, growth, and harvest mirrored the cycle of birth, life, and death. With this newly developed knowledge, Neolithic peoples transformed how they lived and how they died.

Archaeologists continue to debate how long it took for the introduction of farming to lead to the grand development of large-scale architecture. University of Reading archaeologist Richard Bradley has written that ancestor rituals eventually permeated Neolithic society, ultimately resulting in the monumental cairns that now pepper the landscape of Scotland.

These cairns follow a basic plan of an internal chamber accessed by a passage and topped by a dome of stones. The most generic terms for such a structure are *passage grave* and *chambered cairn*, with simple round cairns overwhelmingly the most common style, although builders put up many variations on the round theme. Tor cairns enclose and may cover a large rocky outcrop. Stalled cairns, which I long thought meant that they hadn't been finished, have multiple stalls, formed by vertical slabs projecting from the chamber's walls. Heel cairns resemble a boot heel in shape, rounded with one flattened end. Horned cairns look like a square with rounded points, or horns, projecting out from the corners. Long cairns are wider and higher at the front than at the rear. And finally, ring cairns have a round central chamber but no access passage to it.

Archaeologists have studied chambered cairns for more than two hundred years, but only in the past few decades have extensive excavations allowed scholars to understand the complex building methods. One estimate calculated that, on average, a cairn in the Orkney Islands took 2,985 worker hours to construct.* The builders had to design the cairn, which could involve travel to other cairns to get ideas; clear the ground, which might include burning vegetation and leveling the site; locate and quarry stone, which might involve several sites; transport the stone, some of which could weigh several tons and might require the construction of some sort of road; place the stone, which necessitated cutting wood for levers and platforms; and cover the entire structure in boulders, which could number in the thousands.

For the core, builders placed vertical orthostats up to six feet long. The number depended on the size of the chamber, with a minimum of three and generally many more. In some cases, orthostats are the only part of the cairn that survives. Smaller stones filled the spaces between the orthostats. If the builders did not use orthostats, most likely because the local geology precluded it, they made the walls of stacked horizontal blocks. Chambers ranged in size from less than ten to more than eighty-five feet long.

Roofing the chamber required the elegant solution of a corbelled vault. In this technique successive layers of stone rest atop each other, with each course extending slightly beyond, or oversailing, the one below. Eventually the gap narrows enough to allow small slabs to roof the vault. (If you have ever tried to build a roof with Lego blocks, this is the method you probably used.) To transfer more of the stress, and precipitation, to the outer part of the vault, builders often tilted the layers slightly up toward the center by placing small stones under the corbel slabs. In addition, on well-made vaults, the corners of the corbel stones touched and, over time as the cairn settled, the corners would lock against each other, further strengthening the structure.

---

* In *Land and Society in Neolithic Orkney*, David Fraser used the size of the cairn to determine the number of hours it took to build a cairn. The smallest-volume cairn, at 1,695 cubic feet, required 672 hours; the largest, at 34,396 cubic feet, took 13,636 hours. This compares with an estimated 30 million hours to build Stonehenge.

At the same time that the vault rose, the builders had to add material on the outside to counterbalance the rising corbels. These tail stones helped give what is called the core-cairn its characteristic pyramid-like external shape, usually two to three times high as wide. The tallest vaults rose up more than fifteen feet high.

The passage connecting the chamber and the outside also incorporated orthostats, with horizontal lintels substituting for corbelling such that a flat roof covered what was often the entrance corridor. Because the passages had to support the weight of the core-cairn, they were narrow, averaging between twenty and thirty inches wide. The longest ones extended for up to thirty feet. To draw attention to the narrow passage, builders often framed the doorway with oversized lintels and orthostats.

Finally came the cairn, the pile of stones that covered the entire structure. The cairn could be any size and shape because it provided no structural support. Archaeologist John Barber, who has extensively studied the construction method of Neolithic cairns, wrote in his contribution to *Vessels for the Ancestor* that this allowed the builders to "express changes in fashion, religion, or liturgical practice...[which] is reflected in the strangely ephemeral nature of the structures used to bulk out and form the external cairn."

One of the best places to see Barber's observation put in practice is at the stunning three-cairn complex of Balnuaran of Clava, about five miles east of Inverness, Scotland. Built around 2300 to 2000 BCE, at the end of the Neolithic, Balnuaran consists of two nearly identical single-chambered cairns and one ring cairn. Each round structure measures about fifty-five feet across and looks like a donut, though the chambered cairns have a thin slice, or passage, connecting the hole to the outside. A circle, or kerb in British parlance, of large upright boulders makes up both the inner and outer edges of the cairns. Rocks and rubble fill the space between the kerbs, which act as structural support. At one time, corbelled roofs covered the chambers, but they collapsed at some point in the past. (The ring cairn appears never to have had a roof.)

These cairns were more than simply places to house the dead. By using colored rocks and variably sized kerbstones, and by orienting the chamber access passages to the setting midwinter sun, the builders were able to record time and to connect the living and the dead. Consider the red kerbstones on the southwest side of the cairns and the white mica-rich kerbstones on the northeast, which have the effect of making the cairns glow red in the setting sun and twinkle at sunrise.* In addition, on the southwest cairn —the one most in line with the setting sun —nearly 70 percent of the boulders that cap the cairn are red. It still is quite a sight to watch the cairns shimmer in the setting sun.

Further emphasizing the celestial connection, the kerbstones increase in size to the southwest, so that a person approaching from the northeast would have the impression of the cairns growing in scale from the rear to the entrances to the passages. This pattern repeats itself in the inner kerbs, too. The builders also changed the shapes of the kerbstones, with taller ones having rounded tops and shorter ones pointed tops. When Richard Bradley led an extensive study of the cairns in the 1990s, he concluded in *The Good Stones* that the "sequence of size and shapes embodied in each of the stone circles stood for the progress of the seasons over the course of the year."

Inside the chambers, out of the sun, a person would have noticed the precise alignment of the cairns too. Midwinter sunsets would have been the only time that light pierced the passages and illuminated the red inner kerbstones. Plus, a person standing in the northeast cairn and looking down its passage would have seen the sun setting on top of the southwest cairn at the exact spot where its profile intersected the horizon.

Clearly the builders at Clava took the time to give each structural element a symbolic meaning. By aligning the monument with the never-ending movement of the sun, the builders hoped to cement an unbroken cycle of life and death. Furthermore, as Bradley and others have noted, a focus on the winter solstice and the time of increasing daylight affirmed and strengthened the concept of rebirth, not just for the natural world but also for the dead. Together these powerful concepts would have united the community.

Building an elaborate cairn of stones could also result in unforeseen long-term consequences. At the Point of Cott, a long, horned, stalled

---

* The red rocks are often the Devonian-age Old Red Sandstone, quarried from banks along the nearby Nairn River. The white stone is granite and the gneiss glacial erratics, also found nearby.

cairn on the Orkney island of Westray, John Barber found that the builders enclosed the core-cairn in a series of "onion-skin" walls, which left
open voids, or rooms, between the walls. In a paper for the Scottish Trust,
he noted that birds, otters, and rabbits had nested in the voids. Additional
remains included thirty-six talons from large birds of prey, skeletal parts
from thirteen people, macerated fish bone, and the broken foot of a cow,
trapped between two walls. Like small trailside cairns, the building of the
chambered cairn had created a habitat used by the local animals.

Archaeologists know little about what happened in the cairns and why.
How long was an individual cairn in use? Were the dead buried in them
soon after passing or transported in after the body had time to decay? Did
everyone have access to the dead or was there an elite class who handled
the dead? Why are animal remains often found in the cairns? Did people
believe in some sort of afterlife?

With new analyses in the past few decades, a picture has begun to
emerge that Neolithic people appear to have treated their dead in one
of two ways. At Midhowe on Rousay Island, in one of the more massive
stalled cairns (with twenty-two stalls), excavators found twenty-five individuals ranging from infants to adults. Complete, articulated corpses had
been placed on stone benches within the stalls. Most were in a sleeping
position, their backs against the wall and legs drawn up. This practice is
known as direct interment.

In contrast, on the Orkney island of South Ronaldsay, more than
340 individuals have been recovered from the unusual cairn of Isbister.
Isbister consists of a central stalled chamber with two structurally distinct
end rooms and three side cells. Scattered throughout the main chamber's
floor and shelves were heaps of skulls and bones. Each cell also contained
a hoard of skulls, which "just looked as though they had been bowled
in," wrote lead excavator John Hedges. He concluded that the bodies
had been excarnated, whereby a corpse is placed in a temporary grave or
exposed to the elements until no soft parts remain. Following decomposi-
tion, the living collected the dead's remains and put them deeper in the
cairn or took them to another site.

But in a provocative report, archaeologist Stuart Reilly argued for a middle ground: that processing the dead involved multiple stages. In the initial stage, fully articulated corpses were directly interred in a cairn either on a shelf or in a passage. After the soft parts had decomposed, the bones were moved either to a more central point in the cairn or to another cairn, and then moved once again. Reilly hypothesized that on the isle of Rousay, the bones advanced in elevation to subsequently higher cairns. Each level up translated to fewer but seemingly more important bones, such as the skull, femur, and tibia. In particular, noted Reilly, skulls received special treatment, often ending up in a prominent location, implying that the "community must have held them [the people arranged this way] in great reverence."

Animals may also have played a role in the death ritual. Excavations uncovered more than fifty domestic and wild species within cairns. At Isbister, the high concentration of an undesirable food item—sea-eagle bones—led Hedges to hypothesize that the birds served a totemic purpose. In contrast, Colin Renfrew has argued that animals such as sheep, cattle, and deer served the more utilitarian purpose of ritualistic funerary feasting.

No matter how the Neolithic Scots treated their dead, at some point they closed off the cairns to future use. This involved filling the passages with rubble and sometimes also with human and animal bones. In a few cases, slabs or megaliths were moved in front of the access passage to prevent entrance to the inner chamber; and at one Orkney cairn, rock, animal bones, and earth filled the main chamber but not the side cells. The debris had been dropped in through a square hole cut into the roof.

Most of the cairns then simply succumbed to the agents of erosion and slowly moldered. We have some evidence that a few cairns were reused in the late Bronze Age (1200 to 800 BCE) and even one case of Vikings breaking in and leaving behind extensive graffiti during the twelfth century.* Otherwise the cairns appear to have been little touched for century

---

* Surprisingly, the Vikings did little physical damage; they broke in through a hole in the roof, into what must have been an unfilled chamber. They left behind about thirty inscriptions. "The man who is most skilled in runes west of the ocean carved these runes." "Hokon alone carried treasure from this mound." "Ingibjorg, the fair widow. Many a woman has gone stooping in here. A great show-off." "Thorny fucked. Helgi carved."

upon century. Not until the mid-1800s did British antiquaries begin to investigate the cairns; and, as I noted earlier, not until the 1970s did extensive research begin to tackle questions of function and understanding beyond the simpler questions of how big or how many.

The people who built the cairns clearly valued their dead and the rituals associated with death, but why did they choose to erect a structure that looked like, and in fact was, a pile of rocks? The quixotic archaeologist Alfred Watkins, in *The Old Straight Track*, offers a simple answer. Because of the importance placed on what he called *mark-points*—large single stones or piles of stones that designated important travel routes— people ultimately craved to be buried at such places of distinction. In due time, cairns evolved into burial mounds, with the larger structures mimicking the shape of the smaller ones.

Watkins's observation seems logical and reasonable. I don't find it hard to imagine people of the Neolithic, if not people many thousands of years earlier, erecting cairns to mark trails and important places. Few structures probably carried as simple and widely understood a meaning as cairns. What more potent way could one honor the dead than to bury someone in such a symbolic structure? Yet another way that cairns serve as a marker not just for the living but for the dead as well.

Apacheta

6.

TRAILSIDE SHRINES

Within days there was a cairn... The last I saw, it had grown higher than a man, and still the Wampanoag came, one by one, placing stone upon a stone... The stones had a kind of inner radiance that answered to the sun's changing light at different times of day. It seemed a speaking sort of monument, unlike the mute gray headstones in the English burying ground.

— GERALDINE BROOKS,
Caleb's Crossing

While traveling on November 3, 1734, to establish a mission at what would become the town of Stockbridge in western Massachusetts, Reverend John Sergeant and his interpreter, Ebenezer Poopoo-nuck, passed by a large heap of stones. Sergeant estimated its size at "ten cart loads" and noted in his diary that it had been thrown together by Indians as it "used to be their custom, every time one passed by, to throw a stone on it."

Upon inquiring as to why they placed the stones, Sergeant was told that the Indians did so because "their fathers used to do so, and they do it because it was the custom of their fathers." Poo-poo-nuck added that he supposed that the practice was an expression of gratitude to the supreme being in thanks for allowing them to reach this spot again. To Sergeant, such tales were "childish fables . . . which show us how easily men brought up in ignorance are imposed upon, and should, methinks, excite us the more to pity them."

A year later, an anonymous letter writer provided a slightly different take on the Stockbridge cairn. Each person who passed the pile added a stone to honor the first sachem, who had died after the Indians had moved into the area. The local chief, Konkapot, agreed that the cairn commemorated a long-dead chief. He also stated that new stone was added to keep the marker distinct because it designated a boundary with the Mohawks. "The Muhecunnucks being entitled to have all the country for their hunting ground within one day's journey in every direction from said pile," wrote the anonymous author.

By the late 1700s the area was called Monument Mountain, in honor of the pile of rocks. The cairn measured six to eight feet in diameter and was shaped like an obtuse cone, wrote Reverend Timothy Dwight, who passed by in 1798. Made of small stones of flint, it sat on a high and solitary spot, on consecrated ground far from any Indian settlement. Unlike Sergeant, Dwight did not belittle the erection of such stone monuments and instead recognized that honoring the dead in this manner had a long tradition near "to the custom of the Israelites."

Little known outside the region, the small heap of stones became famous in 1824 when William Cullen Bryant immortalized it in his poem "Monument Mountain." Now the cairn commemorated a young Indian maiden "bright-eyed with a wealth of raven tresses." Gay in heart was she but it was not to last, for she loved her cousin and such love was deemed immoral. So she did what any young maiden would do in a poem of the romantic era and flung herself in despair from atop the precipice. Bryant wrote:

> And o'er the mould that covered her, the tribe
> Built up a simple monument, a cone
> Of small loose stones. Thenceforward, all who passed,
> Hunter, and dame, and virgin, laid a stone
> In silence on the pile. It stands there yet.

Despite Bryant's colorful telling of a poignant tale of love and loss, by the 1840s vandals had destroyed the cairn. Perhaps they didn't take to his poetry, or maybe the miscreants hoped to find buried treasure. No one knows what they found. A bone or two? More likely they found a bunch of old rocks.*

Such commemorative piles of stone occur around the world. The literature mentions trailside shrines, memorial heaps, luck heaps, sacrifice rocks, liar's mounds, rock mounds, rock piles, wishing piles, wayside altars, post offices, and taverns. (I never found the origin of *tavern*. It appears limited to New England.) They all share a singular characteristic: they are, or were, made by travelers adding one stone at a time.

Depending on the tradition, additional stones might be gathered nearby; come from a favored spot, such as one's home; or get carried from the base of the climb if the cairn is located at a high point. American anthropologist Victor Wolfgang von Hagen described rocks ranging from small nuggets up to the size of a hand, though in some cases the offering could be quite large if the carrier hoped to show his or her great strength. How big a cairn gets depends on its age and how often people pass by it. Archaeologists who visited two massive cairns—one in southwest Arizona and one in northeast Argentina—calculated that each contained around fifty thousand stones, which might say more about our fondness for round numbers than for our ability to estimate the quantity of a pile of rocks.

Memorial cairns pop up at crossroads, at seemingly random points on trails, near bodies of water, and in secluded spots far from any path, though they occur most regularly on summits or passes. Archaeologist John Hyslop's monumental study of the vast Inca road system concluded that the road's pre-Columbian builders put up commemorative cairns "where there is some truly monumental ascent or descent that might take a traveler a day or two." He added, though, that a previous researcher wrote that these heaps of stone "do not signify the highest points, but rather places from which one discovers a new horizon, or a major accident of nature." The highest cairns Hyslop found rose on Argentina's Abra del Acay, at more than sixteen thousand feet.

---

* Historian Lion G. Miles, in an article in *The Advocate Weekly*, April 6, 2006, wrote that the monument was much larger than what Dwight described and that it had been destroyed by 1762. He makes a cogent argument, but the basics of the story, in particular Sergeant's observations and Bryant's poem, are attested to in several other sources.

Abra del Acay cairn

No universal reason exists for why people established the tradition of adding stones, and other objects, to these wayside shrines. Some did it to transfer fatigue, some to seek a blessing, and some to propitiate evil. Others deposited stones to honor an event, a person, or a deity.* And some, as in the case of those Native peoples first met by Sergeant, made their offering because of tradition, not fully knowing the details.

Social anthropologist James Frazer boiled the traditions down to a simple reason: transference of evil. In *The Scapegoat*, part six of his monumental and far-ranging analysis, *The Golden Bough: A Study in Magic and Religion*, Frazer looked at how people palm off their troubles onto someone or something else:

> To primitive man the idea of spiritual and ghostly powers is still more indefinite than it is to his civilized brother: it fills him with a vague uneasiness and alarm; and this sentiment of dread and horror he, in accordance with his habitual modes of thought, conceives in a concrete form as something material which either surrounds and oppresses him like a fog, or has entered into and taken temporary possession of his body. In either case he imagines that he can rid himself of the uncanny thing by stripping it from his skin or wrenching it out of his body and transferring it to some material substance, whether a stick, a stone, or what not, which he can cast from him and so being eased of his burden, can hasten away from the dreadful spot with a lighter heart.

Frazer also rejected the ideas of those who thought that the stones were "easy offerings presented by pious but frugal worshippers to ghosts or spirits whose favour they desire to win." He wrote that we can't know the tastes of spiritual beings, but they generally reflect the tastes of mere mortals, and few of us would "be gratified by being set up as a common

---

* In Armenia, a great cairn was built to honor Christian nuns killed by Muslims. Whenever a Tartar passed by, he or she threw a stone on the cairn, but every Armenian took one stone away. In northern California, the Sinkyone people left rocks at a shrine, which had the name "hands lie," a reference to an enemy whose hands and feet had been chopped off and buried at the site. Upon leaving a stone, the supplicant said a prayer wishing that such a fate would not befall him.

target to be aimed at with sticks and stones by everybody who passed within range." More likely, Frazer thought, a practice that started with "magical" implications morphed into one with religious overtones.

Despite Frazer's outdated worldview of "primitive man" (he was writing in 1913), his observations make some sense. We may laugh at the idea of transferring evil, or some other notion or sentiment, to a stone, but many of us "civilized people" have a similar belief. How many of us have burned love letters from a past relationship to rid ourselves of the "evil" contained within? What about the self-help guides that suggest writing down your troubles on a piece of paper and ceremonially casting it away? Or consider the more than 300,000 people who venture each year to Ireland to kiss the Blarney Stone in hopes of gaining the gift of the gab.

What stands out is how dynamic these trailside shrines are in the lives of the people who visit them. People don't just go to the monument and look at it, as we generally do in modern times. For them, the monument is part of a ritual and part of the social fabric of the group. Such monuments are not physically static. Each person who places a stone shapes the monument and thereby adds part of him- or herself to it. These visitors establish a tangible connection that helps inspire and inform their understanding of their place in the world.

Kenestíquai!

How often have you been hiking up some steep and ugly slope and felt drained and listless? In our high-tech modern world, quick rejuvenation is just minutes away. All you have to do is gnaw or swill some chemically enhanced, high-energy performance product. But what did people do before such concoctions? In the Babar Archipelago of Indonesia, they remedied their weariness by hitting themselves with a rock and leaving the stone, which now contained their fatigue, on a cairn. The Huichol of central Mexico would pick up grass and a fist-sized stone, spit on the items, rub them over their knees, cry out *Kenestíquai!* (May I not get tired!), and then lay both on a trailside shrine. One such cairn was known as *Nutíquayë* (He Who Knows How to Cure).

The idea of ridding oneself of fatigue by transferring it to a stone and adding it to a cairn occurs worldwide, one more reason for the abundance of trailside shrines on passes and at the top of steep slopes. James Frazer described variations on this theme from Tibet, Korea, Bolivia, South Africa, and Papua New Guinea. In the United States there does not appear to be any evidence of this ritual on the East Coast, but it did occur among the Pueblo people of the Southwest.

During the 1880s and 1890s, ethnologist Matilda Coxe Stevenson conducted pioneering work among the Zuni Pueblo of New Mexico. Her seminal *Zuni Indians: Their Mythology, Esoteric Fraternities, and Ceremonies* described how Zuni men ceremonially purged their fatigue when preparing for long-distance running races up the sandstone mesas.

> A rocky, picturesque trail leads to the mesa top. A few feet below the summit there is a stone heap 6 to 7 feet high and fully 15 feet at the base, and just before reaching this spot the runner takes a small stone in each hand; he expectorates on the one in the left hand and carries it two, three, or four times around his head from left to right or the reverse and throws it upon the stone heap that he may be rid of his tired breath so that he can start the run with new breath and not lose it.

Now ready to run again, the racer takes the rock from his right hand and uses it as a sort of game piece, moving it with his foot around an elaborate course atop the mesa. His goal: reach a second cairn and toss the stone on it. "When this has been accomplished a man may be sure of winning the race or may risk high wagers on the races," Stevenson wrote.

Tsé Ninájihí

Getting rid of fatigue may be well and good, but it is an immediate solution to a short-term phenomenon. Better yet, when hoping to wrangle a favor from a cairn, is to seek a blessing or to give thanks to a holy spirit, both of which could have more long-lasting impact.

Some of the most detailed descriptions of this practice came from anthropologist Richard Van Valkenburgh, who spent almost twenty years working with the Navajo of Arizona and New Mexico. In the 1940s he knew of more than thirty small shrines that dotted the region's old trails. According to tradition, the first cairn was made by Hasch'ethi (Talking God) on Ch'oln'I'ih (Gobernador Knob in northwest New Mexico) and decorated with white shell, turquoise, abalone, jet, and carnelian. Joining Talking God was Hasch'ehogan (House God), who erected his own cairn of twigs and stone, saying, "We will call this *tsé ninájihí* [where stones are repeatedly placed]." The cairns were made for the Navajo "so that they would have good fortune on their journeys," wrote Van Valkenburgh.

When encountering a tsé ninájihí, a Navajo laid a fresh twig on the pile, covered it with a rock—placed on the side of the cairn in the direction pointed toward one's destination—and made a prayer. Van Valkenburgh translated one prayer:

> Placing rocks, Male One.
> Placing rocks, Female One.
>
> Everywhere I go, myself
> May I have luck.
> Everywhere my close relatives go
> May they have their luck.

The first two lines come from the Blessing Way ceremony, from the part of the prayer for Talking God and House God. Knowing these lines, wrote Van Valkenburgh, would help make the prayer stronger. Additional strength came when supplicants put turquoise or other sacred stones on the cairn. Certain items, however, brought dire misfortune. Burned rocks and anything struck by lightning or whirlwinds were forbidden, as were items touched by a snake or bear. And one only made the offering when heading out, never when on a return trip.

Navajo still continue this practice, according to cultural geographer Stephen Jett. Most of the piles are smallish, under three feet tall, but some are up to seven feet high. The Navajo he spoke with said that there were no rules for where a shrine had to be, though Jett noted that he had usually seen them "at or near the heads of steep trails or steep parts of trails."

High-Country Rocks
Not all trailside shrines are the product of multiple people adding stones. For the Yurok of northern California, building a cairn was part of an individual ritualistic practice. Nearly all such rock stacks or cairns were found in the high mountains, either on summits or on trails through the peaks. The builders generally transported the rock up to the site, often from the Klamath riverbed far below. Ferrying the stone was part of the ritual, as well as a sign of discipline.

In the late 1970s, anthropologist Joseph Chartkoff located more than 326 rock stacks, each consisting of one to four flat stones. When climbing a traditional trail to a sacred peak, individuals would fashion a rock stack and light a fire of cedar twigs or sacred tobacco. In addition to standing in the cleansing smoke, they would recite purification prayers. On the return route, the rock stacks served as a guide helping the "ritualist return home, since after spending up to ten days in fasting, dancing, vigils, and sleeplessness, the ritualist's normal perceptions may be adversely affected." High-elevation cairns differed from rock stacks by consisting of more pieces, from six to more than seventy. Chartkoff found only sixty-three of the larger piles.

Building the rock piles high in the mountains was central to the ritual. Chartkoff noted how communal activities that occurred in the lowlands were "manifestations of acquired powers." In contrast, ritualists traveled to the high country to acquire or renew powers, which enabled them to safeguard their secret rituals. Once a person had acquired powers, he or she could return to the community and help others.

Maledictory Lapidation
Fear can be a powerful motivator, either making us commit acts we shouldn't or not act when we should. James Frazer clearly acknowledged and drew upon this concept when he formed his ideas on the transference of evil.

A CAIRN AND THE BORDER PATROL

Winding through organ-pipe cactus, saguaro, and cholla, Arizona State Route 85 runs from Interstate 8 to the Mexico border. In the early 1980s, US Border Patrol agent John Sanford regularly drove the desolate two-lane blacktop. One day he noticed a small cairn near the road. It stood next to a mile-marker sign several miles north of the border. "I drove that route daily and hadn't noticed the cairn before so figured that someone had put it there to remember something," the now retired Sanford told me.

He pulled over. Footprints clearly led out and back from the cairn. Following them, Sanford came to small clearing a few hundred feet from the road. With a stick he began to dig down into the soft sand. About a foot deep he hit a white pillowcase. Expecting it to be drugs or alcohol (he once found eight cases of Budweiser —still icy cold), he pulled it out and found a Ruger Bearcat, a collectible handgun.

He could have taken it and no one would have been the wiser, but he chose a different tactic. "I got a piece of paper and wrote 'Big Brother is watching,' rolled it up and stuck it in the charge hole of one of the cylinders," Sanford says. He then put the gun back in the pillowcase, reburied it, and walked back to the road. He left the cairn standing.

He wrote that common practice has been to put up cairns at places of violent death, referring to such cairns from Armenia to Venezuela. For some, adding a stone to the cairn helped contain the ghost or spirit of the victim, who could be hostile or vengeful to passersby. For others, a stone offering was sign of respect; to not add one might lead to one's own death. Baganda women of Uganda had another fear. They threw sticks or grass on a grave of a suicide, a twin who died, or a child born feet first so that the ghost of the dead would not enter into the women, impregnate them, and be reborn. The practice applied to all women, no matter their age or marital status.*

The Dyak of Borneo were less concerned about death than about the truth. When someone was lied to, that person would build a *tugong bula*, or "liar's mound," next to the fibber's house, saying, "Let anyone who does not add to this liar's heap suffer from pains in the head." Failure to make an offering, they believed, would result in supernatural punishment.

Sometimes the transference of evil required more than simply placing a rock on a mound. In 1835, an Englishman in what is now Lebanon was traveling along a coastal road when his Native porters stopped to pick up a handful of stones, urging him to do the same. They soon arrived at a conical heap of rock standing in the road. The Brit's companions immediately began to hurl their stones with great vengeance at it, while also cursing vehemently at a robber and murderer who had been killed and buried on the spot fifty years earlier. The traveler wrote that "this custom of maledictory lapidation" prevailed widely throughout the East, though he did not mention whether cursing was required.

Apacheta

The most spectacular, and most studied trailside shrines, are those found along the twenty-five thousand miles of the Inca Road. By the tail end of the Incan Empire in the late 1500s, roads and paths spread through what is now Ecuador, Peru, Bolivia, Chile, and Argentina. Many of the routes wound up and across the Andes Mountains. Still in existence in many areas today, the stone shrines are known as *apacheta*, a word derived from the Quechua for "carrying or having something carried."**

* Bagandans used sticks because stones were rare in Uganda, according to missionary John Roscoe, who wrote of the Baganda in 1911.

** It is sometimes written *apachita*. Other terms include *cotorayaq rumi*, meaning "rock pile"; *tocanca*, a form of the word "to spit," in reference to people spitting coca leaves on the shrines; and *camachico*, meaning "governor" or "commander." Deeper meanings were also applied to *apacheta*, including one from sixteenth-century chronicler Garcilaso de la Vega, whom Carolyn Dean quotes as writing that it implies "we give thanks and offer something to the one who enables us to carry these burdens and gives us health and strength to scale such rugged slopes as this."

Rocks were, and are, the primary item to add to an apacheta, but the range of offered goods is astounding. It includes eyebrow and eyelash hairs, flowers, twined straw, coca wads, sticks, maize, old sandals, feathers, fine cloth, animals, and possibly, in one case, a child. A site may contain one or more cairns, often with a single large one and many, perhaps personal, three- or four-stone shrines. John Hyslop reported that the biggest cairns could consist of millions of stones, each one an offering for some sort of blessing.

Not all of the apacheta were mere piles of stone. Art historian and archaeologist Carolyn Dean has noted that they ranged from simple piles to masonry pyramids to one that consisted of a vertical monolith rising out of a wall of masonry. These more formal apacheta are highly unusual. They are also the only ones depicted in extant illustrations from the 1600s. The pyramid and the monolith appear in watercolors from 1590, one of which depicts a priest (labeled as a wizard) in supplication on his knees in front of the monolith offering coca leaves, feathers, and a child. Dean concluded that the Inca "may well have had a hierarchy of apacheta," where some were "the focus of elaborate state-conduced rites with copious offerings of the most valued kind."

Dean further contends that the Incans may have held apacheta in greater esteem than previously thought. Not only were the apacheta a place to make an offering, they were also objects revered by the Incans, who viewed them as embodying the landscape where they were erected. Apacheta were the "miniaturized petrescence of spirits associated with Andean topography," Dean wrote. In other words, the mountains are actually present in the apacheta, comparable to the belief of Roman Catholics that Jesus is present in the host at Eucharist.

When the Spanish arrived, however, they didn't cotton to what they believed to be idol worship. In 1567, the provincial council in Lima condemned the practice of making offerings to apacheta as superstitious and ordered priests to "strive for disappearing and destroying completely those adoratories." The council did allow priests to leave the apacheta standing if they felt the piles were decent and if they placed a cross on them. It is unclear what justified a "decent" apacheta, but the locals generally ignored such mandates.

But why stone? Why not build commemorative cairns of sticks or bones? Some people did, but for the most part they chose, and often went out of their way to find, rock to make an offering with. The reason is no more complicated than the universality of stone. It is easy to pick up and comes in an infinite number of shapes, sizes, and colors. Once placed on a shrine, stone will not blow away, erode, decay, or suffer in foul weather, at least in human time periods. Nor will anyone covet it or steal it, which does not mean that cairns last forever. A ranger at El Malpais National Conservation Area in northern New Mexico told me that cows and other wildlife like to rub against cairns, which occasionally knocks over the piles. More than animals, though, people are the primary destroyers of cairns.

There is something else about stone though. "Above all, stone *is*," wrote philosopher Mircea Eliade. To primitive man, nothing was more basic nor more noble than stone. Through its hardness, its power, and its permanence, stone "transcends the precariousness of humanity," Eliade wrote. Nor was stone of the profane world but of the sacred world. He cautioned, however, that men did not love stone because it was stone but because they could ascribe to it certain values and feelings: "Men have always adored stones simply in as much as they represent something *other* than themselves."

Our ritualistic use of stone occurs in part because stone is such a benign material. Unlike animate objects, stone has no personal history. It has no feelings or sentiments. It does not change. It just is, and thus we find it easy to ascribe a stone with a value, to make it sacred, to give it the capacity to possess a trait that can help or hinder. And by adding our stone to others, we reaffirm and get confirmation of this belief.

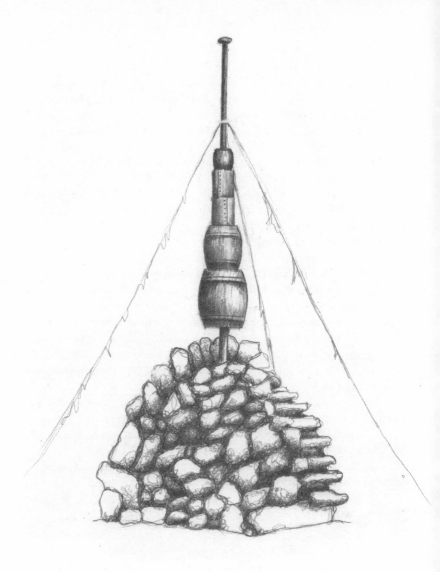

Franklin's cairn, Beechey Island, 1875

7.

EXPEDITION CAIRNS

The Scottish word "cairn" is almost synonymous with explorer. Wherever he goes
we find his cairn, or at least we should find one; *for it and the enclosed record is
the explorer's only proof that he has actually visited that spot* [italics his]. Man may
come and go, but what proof have we that he reached that particular point unless
man follows and finds evidence of the visit?

—DONALD MACMILLAN,
How Peary Reached the Pole

The world's most extensive search for cairns began in the
summer of 1848. Three years earlier Sir John Franklin had
sailed from England to find the Northwest Passage, the nearly mythological water route through the Arctic. Franklin had achieved fame in
the 1820s for two epic expeditions to the Arctic and now led a pair of
ships, the *Erebus* and *Terror*, and 133 men across the Atlantic. After
setting sail on May 10, they reached Greenland, continued around the
island's south end, and sailed north into Baffin Bay on July 22. There
they encountered the whaling vessel *Enterprise* under the command of
Robert Martin.

As ship captains are wont to do when they meet in distant waters,
the men chatted about their plans and the local conditions. Sir John told
Martin that he had provisions for five years and that his men were sup-
plementing their stores by hunting seabirds —which tasted like pigeon
—and salting them for storage in casks. When Martin left a week or so
later, Franklin's boats were moored to an iceberg, with the crews still out
decimating the local bird population.

After loading up on avian meals, the *Terror* and *Erebus* continued east, traveling through ice-choked Lancaster Sound, south of Devon Island. Winter weather began to set in by August, and the boats anchored for the season, nearly 600 miles north of the Arctic Circle. On November 6 the sun set, not to rise again until February 5. Temperatures could drop as low as minus 80 degrees Fahrenheit.

No word of Franklin reached England in 1846. By 1847, as other Arctic explorers and Franklin's formidable and wealthy wife, Lady Jane Franklin, grew more and more concerned, the British Admiralty realized it needed to find its lost expedition. They took a three-pronged approach: over land from the south and by boat from both the east and west. None of the search expeditions found any evidence of Franklin, though Lieutenant Francis Leopold McClintock on the HMS *Enterprise* did discover a cairn at the northern edge of Baffin Island. At the cairn, McClintock performed a ritual that would be enacted repeatedly in the search for Franklin: he demolished the stone pile, hoping to find some evidence of who built it and when. This one turned out to have been erected by John Ross, uncle of the commander of McClintock's ship, in 1825 on one of the earliest searches for the Northwest Passage. McClintock then performed a second ritual by making his own pile of rocks and leaving his own note.

The searches continued through 1849, with additional attempts from both the eastern and western Arctic. But 1850 was the year that hunting for cairns, and Franklin, became all the rage. Lady Franklin, the British Admiralty, the US government, and the Hudson's Bay Company outfitted a dozen ships to scour the Arctic. Their names read like a thesaurus entry for earnest ambitions: *Enterprise, Resolute, Intrepid, Pioneer, Investigator, Advance, Assistance,* and *Rescue.* And then there were names honoring people: *Sophia, Lady Franklin, Felix,* and *Prince Albert.*

As the expeditions explored the headlands, bays, and inlets of the dozens of islands dotting the frigid waters west of Baffin, they found, dismantled, rebuilt, and built cairn after cairn. Most were in prominent locations, seeming to say, as one explorer of 1850 wrote, "Follow them that erected me!" Not every mound of rocks, however, was a cairn. In

1852, Robert McCormick, who was a ship's surgeon on one of the vessels searching for Franklin, wrote, "A thick fog coming on, accompanied by snow-drift sweeping over the bay from the northward, and concealing the outline of its shores, I struck across the low land for the ridge which bounds it inland, passing several isolated masses of rock, which, as they appeared through the snow at a distance, so much resembled piles of stones artificially heaped up, that, dwelling as our thoughts constantly did on cairns and memorials, we were frequently—until the eye became familiar with these deceptions—induced to diverge from our course to examine them." Perhaps he would have had clearer vision if he wrote shorter sentences.

Nothing of Franklin's expedition was found until August 23, 1850, when the *Assistance*, under the command of Captain Erasmus Ommanney, dropped a team at Cape Riley on the southwest corner of Devon Island, 300 to 400 miles west of where Franklin had encountered Robert Martin in Baffin Bay. Ommanney's men had gone ashore to erect a cairn at this prominent cliff on a headland when they found bits of rope, tins of meat, and a cairn. "All this created the greatest excitement, and conjecture was rife whence these remains had come," wrote Clement Markham, a midshipman on the *Assistance*. A thorough search showed that Franklin's men had left this mess but no written message. Ommanney's team built their own cairn, topped by a flagstaff and ball, and left. Two days later the US government expedition under command of Edwin De Haven landed at Cape Riley and "discovered" the new cairn, made, as one crew member noted, from a fossiliferous limestone.

Back on their boat, Ommanney and his men sighted another cairn three miles away across a bay, on the summit of Beechey Island. Ascending to the top of the barren island, Ommanney and his men later reported to the Admiralty that they were "racing almost, so eager were we to see what the cairn contained." Carefully pulling the cairn down stone by stone, they found only some loose shot. With pickaxes, they dug into the hard dirt and rock but made little headway. They then rebuilt the cairn, the first of many times that this cairn was rebuilt. So eager, in fact, were Ommanney's crew they didn't even notice the abundance of artifacts just a mile north on the island.

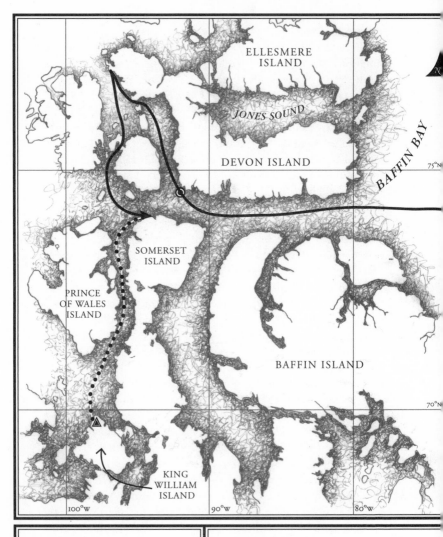

THE FRANKLIN
EXPEDITION

— Known route, 1845
•••••••• Presumed route, 1846
◉ Beechey Island
▲ Victory Point cairn

Four days later, after five of the expedition vessels had joined together at Beechey Island, less eager searchers found the artifacts, including another cairn, on the rocky expanse that ran along Beechey's northern edge and connected to Devon Island by a tombolo (a gravel bar bridging an island to the mainland). The cairn consisted of 600 to 700 bright-red meat tins made by Goldner's in London. The company had supplied Franklin with more than 20,000 tins totaling sixteen tons. The cairn measured eight feet high by six feet wide. Limestone pebbles filled each soup can–sized tin.

One of the long-debated conundrums of the Franklin Expedition is whether the lead used to solder the tins had addled the men's brains and led to poor decision making. In 1985, Canadian researchers reported unusually high lead levels from a Franklin Expedition crew member's bones. Subsequent reports have supported this analysis, but since no intact cans from Franklin's expedition have been found, no one has been able to test them as the exact source of the lead. Some, though, point to the fact that Goldner's had to rush the delivery of the tins, which resulted in the lead in the solder leaking into the food. For example, a 2009 study by researchers at McMaster University showed "off the scale" lead levels from a four-inch-diameter lid from a can of soup found on Dealy Island. The tin, however, was not from the Franklin Expedition but from a search party of that era. Other researchers have argued that the canned foods made up only a small proportion of what the expedition crew members ate, so the tins couldn't have had that great of an effect on the men. In 2008, Franklin Expedition aficionado William Battersby rejected the idea of poisoned tins entirely and instead blamed the *Erebus*'s and *Terror*'s water-distillation system for the lead.

More germane to Franklin, and I suspect more interesting to the men who found the cairn of tins, were the remains of a carpenter's shop, an armorer's forge, and three graves. Two of Franklin's men had died in January 1846 and one three months later. The search teams also located a pair of mittens weighted down by stones; the remnants of a garden bordered in moss, poppies, lichens, and anemones; a tub where the men could wash; and a shooting gallery, with a large tin marked "Soup and

Bouilli" as the target. It wasn't clear if this tin was chosen for size or taste. Clearly the *Erebus* and *Terror* had anchored in this protected bay during the winter of 1845–46. The discovery prompted an even greater search for cairns.

The British are well known for exploring the world, but what they really did was travel around and stack stones. They heaped up rocks in the barren hills of the Egyptian desert, high in the Himalayas, and deep in the jungles of India. Perhaps the first tangible accomplishment the English made in the New World was when Martin Frobisher built a cairn atop a small Arctic island in 1577, sounded a trumpet, and knelt in prayer. The Brits were not alone. Explorers across the centuries have left their mark by erecting a pile of rocks. It may be the one feature uniting world exploration. Whether the explorers discovered new lands, froze to death, ate their boots for survival, got hopelessly lost, or boringly made it to their destination and back again, they built cairns.

A second cairn tradition has been to leave behind an additional token of one's presence. When Sir Richard Burton built a cairn atop Africa's Mount Cameroon (then called Victoria) in 1862, he placed a couple of pages of *Punch* magazine and a list of those who had attained the summit in a sealed canister. Burton took the typical approach of making sure that those who came later knew exactly who had beaten them to that spot. That was what building an exploration cairn was often about: I was here first. Burton later wrote that "to be first in such matters is everything, to be second nothing."* Nor was it unusual for the cairn builder to note that he was the first person to visit the spot, even if he had been led there by a Native guide.

Not content simply to be first and let others know, Captain James Cook exploited the tendency of travelers to stop and examine man-made objects in out-of-the-way places—he embellished the cairns he built on his three explorations of the Pacific Ocean between 1768 and 1779. For example, when he visited New Zealand in 1770, he built a cairn on the

---

* In modern times, getting to a spot first still matters. For some, one of the great frustrations of hiking or exploring is thinking you are the first to reach a spot only to find a cairn. As one friend told me, "It's like finding a pile of litter. It ruined my experience."

summit of a small island off the northeast coast of the country's South Island. Within the stones he placed a coin, beads, and musket balls, items that would let later visitors know that a European had erected this monument. His crowning touch was to hoist the Union Jack atop the cairn. Cook was not only first but he, or at least his king, now owned this property. In his notes Cook wrote, "I dignified this Inlet with the name of Queen Charlottes Sound, and took formal possession of it and the adjacent lands in the name and for the use of his Majesty."

Did no one live in this area? Was there no name for the quiet bay of water? What was Cook thinking? His men had been trading for the previous week or so with the Maori who inhabited the bay and its surroundings, including the island where Cook had built his cairn. The Maori called the sound Totaranui, the "place of big totara trees." But this was the age of British exploration and the Crown's agents asserted their right to take what they wanted. Cook also exacted a promise from the Maori to never pull down the cairn. In return he gave them silver threepence coins, dated 1763, and spike nails inscribed with the king's mark.

I don't mean to single out Cook. His actions were no different than those of other British explorers or explorers from any other country. All felt they had the right to claim newly discovered land, at least "newly discovered" in their eyes, and to build a cairn to show their ownership. Such exploration cairns can be thought of as the advance markers of the oncoming onslaught of imperialism. First came the explorers and their modest monuments, followed by adventure seekers, gold diggers, speculators, and colonists. In the case of the British, you eventually ended up with a vast empire where a cairn was always in sight of the setting sun.

The discoveries of the Franklin Expedition's cairns, graves, and bathtubs on Beechey Island reinvigorated the search for the missing party, particularly around the Beechey cairn. Standard practice dictated that if you did not place information in the cairn, then it should be buried a certain distance away, which Ommanney oddly did not know when he made his initial discovery. Although searchers returned to the cairn, and sifted every inch, they found nothing from Franklin. They did so much damage that a completely new cairn had to be erected on the site.

As time passed a sense of despair revived old rumors. In 1848, the whaling ship *Prince of Wales* had spotted a cairn in Jones Sound, the strait on the north side of Devon Island. Supposedly the whalers had seen footprints in the mud as well as the blackened remains of a fire circle, but they had not stopped to examine the site. People speculated that the *Erebus* and *Terror* had sailed around the west end of Devon Island, continued up to its northwestern tip, and turned east down Jones Sound, more than 400 miles distant. Initially the Admiralty rejected an application to seek out the cairn, but in 1852, with the urging of Lady Franklin, Robert McCormick set out to search for the mysterious Jones Sound cairn.

As the expeditions spread across the Arctic in search of Franklin, cairns proliferated like rabbits. Some went up quickly, such as one that took just forty-five minutes to assemble. But another took ten days to build and measured 15 feet high and 15 feet wide at the base. A 35-foot-tall flagstaff adorned with five casks and topped by a black ball poked out of this cairn. One man who saw the monument estimated that it contained forty-two tons of rock. Even larger was a cairn 16 feet high painted red with a white cross.

Years passed and no additional tangible sign of Franklin's men turned up. In 1854, however, explorer John Rae made a troubling discovery. An Inuit man named In-nook-poo-zhe-jook told Rae that a "party of kabloonans [whites] had died of starvation." In the spring of 1850, the Inuit saw about forty men pulling a boat and sledges. They appeared to be short of provisions and, later the same season, the Inuit found the corpses of some thirty of them. In his report to the Hudson's Bay Company, Rae wrote, "From the mutilated state of many of the bodies and the contents of the kettles, it is evident that our wretched Countrymen had been driven to the last dread alternative—cannibalism—as a means of prolonging existence."

Victorian England would not believe Rae's story. "It has not yet been made clear to us how Englishmen well supplied with clothing and ammunition should not be able to live where any other human beings can subsist," snorted the *Athenæum*. Charles Dickens wrote in his newspaper *Household Words* that the "Esquimaux" couldn't be trusted; given their "covetous, treacherous" nature they had probably set upon Franklin's men.* (We now know that Englishmen could eat one another. Subsequent Inuit reports provided additional descriptions of cannibalism, and in a 1997 study in the journal *Arctic*, an international team reported that of nearly four hundred bones from the Franklin Expedition, more than one-quarter of them had cut marks on them, clear evidence of human and not animal consumption.)

Despite the disavowal of cannibalism, the British Admiralty accepted that many if not most of Franklin's company had died, and it refused to fund any additional search expeditions. Again, Lady Franklin stepped up, with the aid of £3,000 from public subscriptions, and purchased and outfitted a refurbished yacht, the *Fox*. Veteran Arctic explorer Francis Leopold McClintock would lead another expedition. He left England in July 1857, got stuck in ice for the winter west of Greenland, sailed free in April 1858, and spent the winter of 1858–59 in Bellot Strait, about two hundred miles south of Beechey Island.

Honoring Lady Franklin's wishes to search the area where the Inuit had reported seeing survivors from her husband's expedition, McClintock sent out two sledge teams, drawn by dogs and men, to head south from the *Fox* on April 2, 1859. The temperature hovered down around 30 below Fahrenheit. Sledding together the teams covered about 160 miles until they reached Cape Victoria, directly across a frozen bay from King William Island, a spot visited by several explorers in the 1820s and 1830s. McClintock continued south along the east coast of the island, with his second-in-command William Hobson traveling to the west coast. Throughout their travels, the men encountered Inuit, all of whom had items—such as spoons, files, and buttons—from the Franklin Expedition.

On May 24, McClintock found a cairn and then another. Neither contained any message. The next day he and his crew discovered the partially buried skeleton and a few personal items of one of Franklin's

---

* Charles Dickens published Rae's original comments and his response in the December 2, 1854, issue of his newspaper under the title "The Lost Arctic Voyagers."

company. Again, no written information remained. Continuing along the barren shoreline of King William Island, McClintock hiked up a short slope to a well-known cairn built in 1839 by crews from an earlier search for the Northwest Passage. No message, but then twelve miles farther along the coast they came upon another cairn—with a message from Hobson in it.

Hobson had stopped here on May 19. He had not found any Natives or evidence of a wreck that was supposedly in the area, but he did write in the note that on May 5 he had found several cairns at Victory Point, on the northwest edge of King William Island. Following the usual practice, Hobson and his men used picks to break up the snow- and ice-encrusted piles of limestone boulders. The first cairn had no message. The second, built in 1830 by James Ross, contained a sealed copper cylinder holding a single piece of paper. The page was a standard printed form with space to list the name of the ship, date, latitude and longitude, and a short message. On voyages, ship crews would place the form in a cylinder, toss it overboard, and hope that someone would find it and return it to the British Admiralty.

James Fitzjames, captain of the *Erebus*, had filled in the form found in the Victory Point cairn, and it had been left by Lieutenant Graham Gore and Charles Des Voeus, shipmate:

28 of May, 1847
H.M. ships "Erebus" and "Terror" wintered in the ice in
Lat. 70° 05' N., Long. 98° 23' W.
Having wintered in 1846–7 at Beechey Island, in
Lat. 74° 43' 28" N., Long. 91° 39'15" W. After having ascended Wellington Channel to lat. 77°, and returned by the west side of Cornwallis Island.

Sir John Franklin commanding the expedition.
All well.

Party consisting of 2 officers and 6 men left the ships on Monday, 24th May, 1847.

In dating the form, Fitzjames had erred by a year. The graves on Beechey Island showed that the *Erebus* and *Terror* had spent the winter of 1845–46 at Beechey. Some have speculated that Fitzjames's error is evidence of the deteriorating effects of lead-tainted food. Nevertheless, as McClintock noted in his account of the search expedition, "That winter appears to have passed without any serious loss of life." "But, alas!," he continued, someone else had updated the information on April 25, 1848.

For nineteen months, since September 12, 1846, the *Terror* and *Erebus* had been trapped in ice, said the addendum. The crews had abandoned the boats just three days prior to writing the note. One hundred and five men were alive, under the command of *Terror* captain Francis R. M. Crozier, who had signed the note along with Captain Fitzjames. They planned to venture south on the 26th in search of Back's Fish River, which flowed from the south into the Arctic. By this time, nine officers and fifteen crew had died, including Sir John Franklin, who had perished just thirteen days after the original document had been signed.

Encouraged by Hobson's discovery at Victory Point, McClintock and his small crew proceeded west and north. They soon came upon a twenty-eight-foot-long boat mounted on a sledge. Inside it were two skeletons, partially consumed by some large animal. No journals were found, though the searchers did locate several books of scripture. At the cairns discovered by Hobson, McClintock found extensive remains, including piles of clothes, four heavy cooking stoves, iron hoops, and a case containing twenty-four vials of medicine, but not one scrap of paper.

Running low on food, McClintock stayed for just a day or so before heading back to the *Fox*, where he arrived June 19. Three months later he was in London, soon to become a national hero for leading the exploration that found the note in the cairn. In his narrative of the expedition, McClintock wrote, "A sad tale was never told in fewer words."

No other written remains from the final Franklin Expedition were ever found, though the lost men may have left other papers. Contemporary explorers did find papers under some cairns, but they had faded. In at least one case the Inuit told of finding written material

A WOMAN'S PLACE IS ON TOP

So, it was circa 1983. I was completing the "spring block" with Huxley College, a quarter-long experiential education program that I needed as partial requirement for my environmental education degree. Approximately twenty-five of us took four courses together, such as "Environmental Interpretation," "Writings of American Naturalists," and "Experiential Education," in which we rock climbed, winter camped, river rafted, and so on.

The culminating experience was a sixteen-day backpack in the Pasayten Wilderness in Washington State, which included a three-day solo and an expedition with map and compass. We broke up into smaller groups by drawing names out of a hat. I ended up in an all women's group.

Our group decided to climb 8,334-foot Windy Peak as part of our trip. Several years prior to this, the book *Annapurna: A Woman's Place Is on Top* had come out about the first expedition to Annapurna led by a woman and also by an American. The title of this book became our inspiration for climbing Windy Peak. We got up in the wee hours and made it to the top before the snow got soft.

We were hiking on snow with snowshoes for the entire sixteen-day journey, and cairns were an important part of our wayfinding above timberline. At the top of Windy Peak, we found our last cairn. We knew other groups from our class would be climbing Windy, so we decided to leave them a message. We wrote "A Woman's Place Is on Top" on a little piece of paper, stuck it in a plastic bag, and placed it under one of the cairn rocks. Then we all stripped from the waist up, put the camera on auto timer, and quickly took a chilly topless portrait of our women's group "on Top" of Windy Peak, with the cairn to document our ascent.

One of our fellow groups did find our note in the cairn, and the photo remains a favorite from that time in my life.

LINDA VERSAGE is an educator based in Seattle.

in containers, but they had thrown the writings out because they had no use for them.

For more than 150 years people have traveled to the Arctic looking for signs of Franklin's lost men. They have hiked, paddled, and flown across the icy north. They have used special remote-control underwater probes to seek out sunken ships. They have sought out psychics to divine where the men died. They have dug up skeletons and attempted to determine who had died. And, explorers have continued to seek out cairns, tear them down, and search for clues. The world's most extensive search for cairns continues.

Stacked stones

8.

STACKING STONES

I began rock stacking as a way of honoring an urgent inner soul demand to be
more balanced, quiet, still, and centered. It was time to respond to the call for
equanimity in the various dimensions of both my inner and outer life. I had
heard this call before, but it was not until I began rock stacking that I felt I had
adequately answered the call.

— PEGGY STRINGER,
"An Intimate Exploration of Rock Stacking
as a Sacred Art Form Evoking the Numinous Experience"

About three miles south of Carmel, California, you can find
a singular sign. Diamond in shape and bright yellow with black
words, it reads, GRAVITY AT WORK. The sign is nailed to a Monterey pine
that overlooks a yard of grass, low shrubs, boulders, and a picnic table.
Another sign adorns a tree near the table. It holds a three-panel display
where you learn that you have entered the Gravity Garden, property
maintained by artist Jim Needham.

The garden is free and open to the public. You are welcome to take pictures, walk the grounds, and eat lunch at the picnic table, but Needham
warns you to "move carefully" through the space because of the instabil-
ity of his sculptures. At the bottom of the warning panels, he emphasizes
that neither he nor the landowner are responsible for any injury or damage you might sustain in the garden.

Needham is a master rock stacker. Most of his works of art sit on the
ground, though a few perch on tree limbs. Nearly all of the towers are
made from boulders smoothed by the nearby Carmel River, from which
Needham estimates he has collected at least eighty tons of rock. He has

sorted the cobbles and boulders into piles, some a dull gray, some with veins of white quartz, some of tannish-orange sandstone, and some of speckled gray and black granite.

Dozens of stone stacks grace the garden. One of my favorites consists of three stones. The bottom looks like a salt-and-pepper-colored, classic army helmet. Atop it rests another gray and black stone, this one rectangular and balanced on one of its long narrow sides. The top stone is a perfectly round ball of dark gray with streaks of white. Total height: about twenty-four inches. Nearby stands another shapely stack, fashioned to look like a whale fin with an oblong rock balanced atop it.

Several sculptures are taller than I am and include more than ten cobbles. The biggest sculpture, however, has just two blocks. The larger of the relatively flat blocks of sandstone weighs 6,600 pounds and is roughly rhombus shaped. The lower rock looks like a basketball backboard with a flat bottom, which sits on the ground, and a curved top. "This piece pissed me off," Needham told me. He worked on it for almost twenty-five days before achieving the right balance of just three small points of contact between the two stones. Like many of his stacks of stone, it seems the antithesis of Needham's GRAVITY AT WORK sign.

Needham started stacking stone in 1995 after a series of floods on the Carmel River. Initially, he had simply tossed the stones to clear out some property, but around this time he fell in love. "She was a muse. I wanted to write poems for her," he said. He also started to make small stacks of stone and, being a photographer, he took photos of them for her. He hasn't stopped since. "The rocks kept calling me over. They are incredibly brilliant. I think they bred us to move them," he said.

Building a stack is a full-body experience for Needham. As the rocks shift during what he calls "the dance," he settles the tower with his torso, hands, forearms, knees, and even his head. To find the balance of the rocks he relies on their vibrational energies. "It's all about the lay lines, or energy lines, of the earth, which create a harmony and a synchronicity. It's sort of the Shiatsu of the earth," he told me.

He recognizes that most people don't get this idea. "People don't have balance in their life," he says on his website. "It's a concept foreign to them. Then one day I just said, you know, it's gravity, just gravity at work. And suddenly it became clear to people. Oh, science. I don't have to understand science. That's a rule. . . . And they'd walk away and they'd understand better. They were less confused by it. They were reassured."

Before he began stacking stone, Needham told me, he used to often upset people with his politics. "Now, I can go into schools. People became more friendly. It opened up their hearts," he said. When I asked him if he had had any problems with vandals, he laughed. No one has ever disturbed the Gravity Garden on purpose.

Rock stacking, or rock balancing as some prefer to call their passion, has become something of a fad in the past two decades. You can find dozens of videos posted on YouTube of people stacking stones. You can purchase DVDs, too, of famous stone balancers such as Bill Dan, who, according to his promotional materials, is also "available for conventions, parties, conferences, marketing projects, museum demonstrations, advertising campaigns, TV shows, landscape installations, garden shows, reunions, openings, retirements, weddings, and bar mitzvahs." You can take rock-balancing workshops from nature sculptor Zach Pine and, as befits our modern world, you can download an app for stacking stones.*

Because of the nature of stone stacking, we have no evidence of how long people have practiced this art, though it seems safe to say that it has gone on for thousands of years. One of the few sites with a long history is the Tapsa Temple complex in South Korea. Beginning in the late 1800s, a lone monk, Yi Gap Yong, spent three decades assembling more than one hundred stone towers. He reportedly collected the stones specifically from rivers and stacked them according to Taoist concepts of reality. About eighty remain and consist of either a single column of stones or a conical mound topped by a stone column.

---

* The Stones of Tranquility app promises that it "calms and focuses your mind with beautiful graphics, serene sound and relaxing gameplay. Based on the ancient Zen practice of stone stacking, this game contains no explicit goals, achievements or failures, the reward is the process itself. Take your mind off everyday troubles, skip the next cigarette or just relax. Let the stones provide you with stability, balance and focus on the present."

British artist Andy Goldsworthy is probably the best-known stone stacker of modern times. Many credit, or blame, him for the art form's recent popularity. Always interested in patterns and space, Goldsworthy started creating simple stone stacks in the 1970s, such as a 1978 piece that had a rock shaped like India with its southernmost point balanced at the tip of a rock that resembled a squat South America. As his work progressed, balancing gave way to installations based more on shape, color, texture, and whimsy. For example, he once froze a cairn to the side of a quarry wall, made another cairn all of red rock to enhance sunset light, still another of wet rocks on a dry beach, and finally one of tan rock in order to reflect moonlight.

Like many others who stack stone, Goldsworthy values the ephemeral quality of his work. "I was always interested in seeing work change and decay, but usually as a spectator. Lately the challenge has been not simply to wait for things to decay, but to make change an integral part of a work's purpose so that, if anything, it becomes stronger and more complete as it falls apart and disappears," he writes. His pieces, though, are not truly ephemeral, as he scrupulously photographs all of his work, which has helped make him world famous.

Goldsworthy has inspired so many because he has revealed the possibilities of working with stone as an artistic pursuit. He has made stone beautiful, full of textures, light, and color. A mixture of simple and complex, abstract and geometric, static and dynamic, Goldsworthy's work balances the yin and yang forces within stone.

Nearly every full-time or serious stone stacker offers some sort of explanation about balance. To find the right energy within the stones means slowing down and concentrating. Balancing stones has a calming effect. It is meditative. It centers. It brings peace. As one practitioner wrote, "One cannot make the rocks balance by being assertive, powerful, controlling, manipulative, threatening, yelling, or any other form of intimidation. The rock is obviously completely unaffected by any of this." Obviously.

There may be something to what these rock stackers say. The work of well-known stone balancers is amazing. Many of their sculptures don't seem possible, as if there are unseen forces at work. (Some skeptics think that that force is glue.) The stone stackers use every size and shape of rock, creating structures that look like a fantastic mix-up of Salvador Dali and Dr. Seuss. Some are quite beautiful. Others simply mystify. And many have inspired others to go out and attempt to make their own stacks.

In some areas, however, the proliferation of stone stacks has led to a backlash. Officials in Hawaii have posted signs asking people not to build the piles. A popular tourist map even includes the following statement: "The stones you see stacked along the road are done by visitors who believe there is some significance. There is none."

Stone stacking got to be such a problem in Hawaii that the US Geological Survey's Hawaiian Volcano Observatory condemned the practice. Visitors to Hawaii Volcanoes National Park were prying boulders off of lava flows and disturbing and destroying scientific evidence. "If this practice is not stopped," said the USGS in its *Volcano Watch* newsletter, "our grandchildren may only be able to experience rock piles—and that's a story no one would be proud to pass on. To paraphrase an often-repeated slogan, just say 'no' to rock piles."*

Collecting and piling up stones didn't just damage geologic evidence; as respected community leader Kupuna Pele Hanoa told a local newspaper, it was "akin to sacrilege." Because many sites sacred to Native Hawaiians dotted the national park, she called the rock piles a desecration of Native culture.

Rangers at Yosemite National Park also face an epidemic of stacked stone. Some "rock gardens" contain hundreds of short stacks of rocks, as well as stacks in trees and stacks towering more than six feet tall. A recent one-page handout for park visitors addresses the environmental and safety issues and appeals to people's aesthetic concerns: "Places like Yosemite were preserved to protect natural processes and views of natural landscapes, not as showcases for free-form public art."

People claim that their stacks of stone are "works of art" or attempts to get in touch with nature and that naysayers are just unwilling to understand them and their work. People who object to the cairn epidemic often

---

*The national park's campaign to educate people, along with destroying inappropriate cairns, has led to a drastic reduction in such cairns. The park also benefited from the renewed eruption of lava in 2008 from the Halema'uma'u crater on Kilauea, which resulted in trail closures.

express disappointment at finding evidence of others who have come before them—to which one stone stacker responds that obviously these people aren't getting far enough into the backcountry to experience true wildness, so they have no reason to complain.

To many, erecting personal cairns, whether to mark a route or for some more philosophical reason, is the equivalent of graffiti—an

THE "VILLAGE PEOPLE"

As a climber for the last quarter century, I've long, and with nary a thought, relied on cairns to guide me to and from the summits and cliffs, and I've stacked a few of my own to help others along the way. What a simple pleasure: combing the ground for the perfect, flat-bottomed stones, flipping them over to best match the facets, and then balancing the stack. It takes minutes to build a good, solid cairn but only a second to kick it over, to turn array into disarray. In my misspent youth I more than once took perverse, arrogant pleasure in upsetting "unnecessary" cairns, though I've since corrected my error. As a friend once told me, "Even if *you* don't need those cairns, you never know why someone else put them there."

One day in the late 1980s, three of us were climbing in Box Canyon, a tight, basaltic defile southwest of Socorro, New Mexico. A dry streambed pierces the canyon, filling with water only during flash floods or the summer monsoons, when the biting black gnats become unbearable. Otherwise it's an ever-shifting ribbonwork of sand and water-smoothed cobbles, pretty to behold but tough to navigate. This day, we'd taken a break from bouldering near the up-canyon parking lot when we noticed a forest of slender, elegantly stacked cobble "stone men" in the streambed. We ran down and, unneeded, self-indulgent blight on the natural landscape. Part of the reason many people go into the backcountry is to get away from human influences. They know they are going into previously visited areas, but that doesn't mean they want to be reminded of who came before. A friend told me she doesn't like seeing even one cairn in the backcountry because it reminds her of people. She recognized this was a bit extreme,

like the yahooligans that we were, started kicking them over. Just then an old pickup pulled in. Three deranged characters—a skinny guy with a beard and a giant, waist-holstered Bowie knife, and two spacey hippie chicks, all looking like antagonists in a kill-spree horror flick—lurched our way.

"Hey, what are you doing to our village?" the man demanded. He moved his hand down toward his belt where it hovered by the knife.

"Yeah," said one of the women. "That's not cool. We worked hard on this."

"You guys just go around destroying other people's things?" the guy continued. "You think that's funny? That was our *village*."

Because you couldn't argue with the man's logic, and because he was armed, we took to apologizing…profusely. We even offered to help put "the village" back up, but the trio declined. As we monkeyed around on the boulders over the next two hours, we watched them moving through the wash, re-erecting their stone men. When they'd constructed the village back to whatever specs they were following, they drove away. I never did kick over another cairn after that. Like my friend had admonished, you never know why someone else put it there.

MATT SAMET is a freelance writer and editor in Boulder, Colorado, and the former editor-in-chief of *Climbing Magazine*.

especially when she sees a cairn while hiking on a trail—that has presumably been built by people.

Maybe if there were only one or two stone stacks those who object would be more respectful and accepting. But just as the backcountry cairn critics know that they are most often traveling well-trodden ground, people who erect such towers should recognize where they're building them and know that others, many others, will come later and will follow their example—one stack can quickly multiply into dozens. If getting in touch with nature or your own wildness requires building a cairn or stacking a bunch of stones, consider taking it down when you're finished: those who come after you also may want to get in touch with nature and may not want to see your calling card.

If you head north from Jim Needham's Gravity Garden back to Carmel, you can find a couple of my favorite stone structures: Hawk Tower and Tor House. Poet Robinson Jeffers, who lived in Carmel from 1914 until his death in 1962, hand-built the forty-foot-tall tower and neighboring house. He used boulders that he collected from the beach below, making the buildings seem less man-made than born geologically from the hillside, as if Jeffers had used the nearby cliffs, sea stacks, and outcroppings for blueprints.

They also exemplify the balance one can achieve through working with stone. Before he moved to Carmel, Jeffers's poems were flat, simple, and little appreciated. After taking up residence at his oceanside property and starting on Tor House, he found a voice unique in American poetry. His wife, Una, wrote one of his biographers that "as he helped the masons shift and place the wind- and wave-worn granite I think he realized some kinship with it and became aware of strengths in himself unknown before. Thus at the age of thirty-one there came to him a kind of awakening such as adolescents and religious converts are said to experience."

I think that much of Jeffers's poetry would resonate with those who balance rocks. In "Star-Swirls," published posthumously, Jeffers wrote, "What a pleasure it is to mix one's mind with geological / Time." In another poem, mountains "neither hear nor care, but your presence helps," while in "The Old Stonemason" waves are "drunken quarrymen / Climbing the cliff, hewing out more stone for me." But it is one line that Jeffers wrote in a paean to his beloved Tor House that I think would resound most with the stone stackers: "My fingers had the art to make stone love stone."

Inuksuk

9 ·

CAIRNS, A
WORLD TOUR

She and Lexa proudly tussled up a sizable rock and crammed it into the cairn
the man had under way nearby. The herder came out, saw their achievement and
threw a fit. "What's that doing on there? That is a bad leave!" After he quit raving
and expelled their rock in favor of a smaller one that chinked into place more
readily, the girls grasped that whenever stones were forced to fit together the way
theirs was jammed in, it left trouble when the next stone had to be inserted.

— IVAN DOIG,
Mountain Time

At the most basic level, you can define a cairn as a pile of
rocks. But this definition doesn't do justice to the myriad shapes
and sizes of cairns found around the globe. Nor does it convey the many
reasons that people have built cairns for thousands of years. Yet, when
you see a cairn, whether lovingly built and maintained or slapped up for
a single use, you know what you are looking at. You know that someone
has taken the time to gather rocks and assemble them into a recognizable
shape that carries a specific message.

Each of the following eleven vignettes focuses on a different type of
cairn, either a single structure or a broad category of them. The cairns
range in time from the mythological past through ancient Greece to
modern builders. Some of the cairns are fabled, some sacred, and some
honorific. Some present a conundrum with no clear explanation as to
why they were built. A few are a bit whimsical. Only one marks a trail,
which happens to be the most famous trail in America. Two are made of

ice that has probably not melted since the cairns were erected, but they can no longer be seen. And one type you may not consider to be a cairn; or, at least, these cairns were not made by people.

It is the fundamental aspect of cairns that they convey a meaning understood by so many, which makes them such a powerful resource on the landscape—and an essential part of human culture.

Harri Mutilak: Assertion of the Self

If you drew a map of the United States, including Hawaii and Alaska, on a piece of cardboard, carefully cut along the outline of the map, and then tried to balance the cut-out cardboard on the tip of a pencil, you would find the balance point near Belle Fourche, South Dakota. If you then traveled to Belle Fourche, you would find a visitor center, a walkway lined with flagpoles displaying the fifty state flags, and a twenty-one-foot-wide black granite compass. You would also learn that the National Geodetic Survey has designated Belle Fourche as the official geographic center of the United States, the point at which the entire country would balance if it were a flat plain of even thickness.

The setting is nice, but it is a ruse. Working with folks from the geodetic survey in 2007, the Belle Fourche Chamber of Commerce relocated the official center of the nation from an isolated spot twenty-five miles north of town. The move came about because center seekers had to drive down a gravel road and, according to the *Rapid City Journal*, "swerve around some cow pies and cactus" to reach the original site. Those willing to endure such brown and green challenges would have found a wooden sign noting that, with the inclusion of Alaska and Hawaii in 1959, the nation's center had moved from Smith Center, Kansas, to South Dakota, a distance of about 435 miles.

Intrepid travelers could also have discovered a less geographically intriguing but still thought-provoking sign just up the hill from the old monument. Standing near a narrow cairn of sandstone slabs and behind a chain-link fence, the sign bore the title "Sheepherder's Monuments." It read, "Sheepherder's Monuments or stone Johnnies survive the days of the open range. These stone columns were probably built to indicate distance and direction to waterholes and provided the sheepherder with a pastime while tending his flock."*

Not limited to open range, stone Johnnies graced hundreds, if not thousands, of buttes, ridges, hogbacks, and mesas across the west.** The piles of stone went up everywhere that sheep grazed and sheepherders tended their bands. Others in the West surely built cairns, but no other group had so much free time—primarily alone—to gather rocks and assemble them into long-lasting piles.

No one has traced the origins of this stone-piling tradition, but Basque sheepherders often get credit. The original Basque immigrants came to the West—primarily to California—for gold, not wool. By the late 1850s, however, they had met the fate of most gold seekers and had turned to other pastimes, in their case, sheep. The Basque spread slowly across the West, first to the warm states and then north to the cooler climates of Montana and Wyoming. They were, in the words of historian and novelist A. B. Guthrie Jr., writing in the magazine *Country Beautiful*, "the best of all herders, better than the Romanians, the Irish, [and] the Scandinavians."

The Basque called their stone monuments *harri mutilak*, or "stone boys." Early historians wrote that the sheepherders built harri mutilak out of loneliness or because they had been "sagebrushed," that is, slipped into madness. "I don't think the Basques were that lonely or crazy," Joxe Mallea-Olaetxe, author of *Speaking through the Aspens*, told me. "It so happens that they [harri mutilak] are only found in stony areas and in strategic summits. Are we to believe that the Basques were lonely only on rocky mountain tops?"

* According to Shirley Baughman O'Leary's *Stone Johnnies*, the original center-of-the-nation-site was ten miles west at an "almost inaccessible location off a dirt road." The state of South Dakota then rerouted US Highway 85 to the new site.

** Sheepherder's monuments is the most common term for these cairns. Other terms are rock Johnny, butte marker, and water marker. Very few people I talked with, including folklorists, archaeologists, and former sheepmen, had heard the term stone Johnny. One possible origin for stone Johnny is that it comes from the Basque phrase, stone boy. The earliest reference to this term I could find was in the 1931 United States Geological Survey Bulletin 831, Part B on coal in Montana. About 225 miles north of Belle Fourche is Stone Johnny Hill, North Dakota, the lone geographic feature officially named for these cairns.

He notes that the Basque built harri mutilak to mark range borders, to prevent the mixing of sheep bands, and to aid new herders who didn't know the region. During foggy weather, the stone piles became critical guideposts. Mallea-Olaetxe added that some Basque cairns went up for no other reason than "for a young, well-fed, and rested herder to exercise his muscles."

Built of large, flat slabs, most harri mutilak are less than six feet tall and about three feet in diameter at the base. Mallea-Olaetxe has seen them across the West, with some built in the eastern Sierra Nevada as high as 10,000 feet elevation. The most unusual ones he saw are in northeastern Nevada. Near Jarbridge, he came across a pair, one tall and narrow and one squat. A long narrow stone, flanked by two rounded rocks, rose out of the smaller structure. Mallea-Olaetxe suspected that they were a couple—a larger female and a small, well-endowed male. "The herders were young and horny all the time," he said. "I am not surprised that some very horny fellow built man-woman cairns overlooking the road to Jarbidge."

Only one study has analyzed sheepherder's monuments. In 2011, Wyoming State Archaeologist Mark Miller sent me his research about the ranch started by his great grandfather in 1873. The Miller ranch sheep herd peaked at 40,000 head in the 1880s and by the 1940s had dropped to 6,500 sheep ranging across 170,000 acres of federal, state, and private land. Never idle, the sheep ran on an eightfold cycle of counting, trailing (fall and summer), ranging (summer and winter), shipping, shearing, and lambing, with each cycle dependent on weather, water, food, and shelter.

Winter range was the longest and most challenging part of the cycle. Lasting from October to May, it could be a brutal time with northern storms whipping in extreme cold, wind, and snow. The sheepherders' main concern during this time was to find protected bedding ground where a couple of thousand sheep could weather the storms. Sheltered areas below river terraces, ridges, or hills were the most popular spots. The men could stay warm and watch their sheep below by locating their camp wagon on a high point.

Miller found that winter range was the only time when sheepherders built their cairns, and always on prominent high spots. He concluded that the men had built them for the simple reason of having additional markers to help find their way when returning from grazing sheep during blizzards.

Such practical explanations for why sheepherders piled up stone make sense, but I don't think we can rule out boredom. Living in isolated, desolate spots, they may have seen another person just once every week or two. Their only companions were a dog and bands of unruly, often incredibly stupid sheep. Surely you would want a pastime. Some turned to carving trees, creating elaborate works of self-expression, but many also turned to stone. After all, there are worse ways to while away your time, and if heaping rock upon rock helped prevent a man from drifting into madness, so much the better.

Unfortunately, many stone Johnnies are disappearing from the West or are long gone. In her book, *Stone Johnnies: Vanishing Landmarks of the Lonely Buttes*, Shirley Baughman O'Leary writes that how, during the "Dirty Thirties," people dismantled the cairns and used the stone to build stock dams. Range wars between cattlemen and sheepmen led to further destruction because the cowboys would lasso a monument and pull it down. Other cairns simply disappeared stone by stone for more immediate uses, such as killing a snake, building a fence, or for cement work. One of O'Leary's correspondents, a sheepherder named Tiny Mellott who built hundreds of stone Johnnies, told her scornfully that, in recent times, "city dudes" have arrived, backed up a pickup, and loaded up on stone simply to make a rock garden. Such is the fate of these legacies that A. B. Guthrie Jr. called "an assertion of personality, a testimony of self to the everlasting impersonal."

Of Gods and Cairns

A world away from the American West, about sixty miles southwest of Athens, Mycenae is one of the great archaeological sites of the Bronze Age. More than a century of excavation has unearthed scores upon scores of objects, from golden crowns to bronze swords to elaborate pottery. Amazingly, a handful of items dated at around 1300 BCE pertain to cairns, highlighting a profound connection between people and stone.

Archaeologist Christos Tsountas unearthed the objects in the late 1890s from a dromos tomb, a small enclosure with an entry corridor. One of his finds—a lazuli blue glass-paste plaque about the size of a nine-volt battery—shows a small pile of stones surmounted by a larger object, most likely another stone. On either side of the heap stands a daemon, a being with a deer-like head on a human-like body, pouring a libation on the pile from a sacred ewer. Neither human nor divine, daemons were cult figures that possessed powers over animals and humans.

Describing this plaque in 1947, archaeologist Jacqueline Chittenden wrote, "In the mind of the craftsman who made this plaque the idea existed that a heap of stones was a worshipful thing." The plaque was one of many depictions of cairns made by Bronze Age and early Greek artists. Painting and carving on vases, signet seals, and coins, they depicted stone piles as sacred objects adorned with goats, lions, and palm trees.

But why did the early craftsman worship piles of stones? asked Chittenden. The answer lay in similar objects bearing daemons. In each case, a godlike figure exerts control over the daemons. Chittenden concluded that the daemons were servants to what she called the Master of Animals, or the "heap deity of the Minoans." To the craftsman, the Master of Animals was synonymous with the heap of stones; the deity either pervaded the pile or was immanently connected to it.*

The cult of the cairn did not die out with the decline of the Mycenaean civilization, she wrote. It morphed into the worship of Hermes, the Greek god of travel, literature, and shepherds. Hunters, pastoralists, and wayfarers sought his protection as they traveled because, like the Master of Animals, Hermes controlled the beasts. He also shared a long-standing and direct connection to cairns.

---

* Modern archaeologists no longer accept Chittenden's explanation. They agree that the Mycenaeans used stones in their rituals and that they worshipped the Master of Animals, but they argue that how the craftsmen depicted him in their iconography is not clear.

One of the earliest literary references to Hermes comes from the *Odyssey*. When Odysseus's swineherd, Eumaeus, tells Telemachus, Odysseus's son, of seeing a ship in the harbor, he says, "I was above the city by the hill of Hermes." Greek scholars for more than twenty-five hundred years have defined the original Greek for "hill of Hermes" as a stone heap. Hermes was then "he of the stone heap," a god initially personified by a cairn. Chittenden cheekily bestows upon Hermes the nicknames "the heapy one" and "Old Heapy."

Greek scholar W. K. C. Guthrie offers another explanation for Hermes's name in *The Greeks and Their Gods*. He writes, "To explain the connection of Hermes with the cairns, the Greeks characteristically invented an aetiological myth. When Hermes killed Argos, he was brought to trial by the gods. They acquitted him, and in doing so each threw his voting-pebble (*phethos*) at his feet. Thus a heap of stones grew around him." Henceforth, legend held that travelers who erected cairns would be protected by Hermes, who dwelt within the pile.

Eventually a *hermes*, or *herm*, came to mean a boundary marker, signpost, or milestone. People often built a hermes for protection in front of their houses in Athens. Over time the cairns acquired more human attributes, most noticeably the addition of a phallus, either erect or carved in relief. In 415 BCE, during the Peloponnesian War, protestors dismembered these markers in Athens in what is known as "mutilation of the herms," truly one of the low points in the history of cairns.

Of all the Greek gods, Hermes was the ideal one to associate with cairns. Sure Zeus is mighty, Hera a babe, but what good are those attributes on the trail? Of his many manifestations, Hermes stands out as a protector, a guide, a friend to those in need, even to those who have died. One of his many tasks was leading souls down to Hades.

Again, the *Odyssey* provides a telling account of Hermes, when he appears to Odysseus after the sorceress Circe has turned the wanderer's men into pigs. Hermes comes to Odysseus's aid, saying, "Where are you off to now, unlucky man, Alone, and in rough, uncharted terrain. . . . I will keep you out of harm's way." Certainly a fine way to express what most of us would hope for from a cairn.

CAIRNS

Oboo from Mongolia

One of the world's classic parables involves an elephant and six blind men. Each man is led to an elephant and told to describe what he feels. The one at the leg compares it to a pillar. The one at the tail to a rope, with each subsequent man coming up with a different description. Each is right, showing how the truth depends on what you experience.

A similar claim could be made about the *oboo* of the Mongols.* Piles of stone, often including tree branches, though sometimes made of dirt and snow or, very rarely, dung, oboo dot the landscapes of Mongolia, eastern Kazakhstan, the Buryat Republic in Siberia, and northern China. Depending on which ethnologist you read, oboo relate to shamanist or Buddhist rituals; originate with the death of a young sheepherder, from ideas expressed by Confucius, or because of war councils held by Genghis Khan; entail an animal sacrifice or not; and/or require the erection of from 13 up to 108 cairns, depending upon the variation. As with the elephant, all of these claims are correct, at least for the specific time and place when the researcher visited.

The great variety grew out of religion and geography. Oboo worship can be traced from animistic to shamanist to Buddhist beliefs, each sharing the goal of pleasing local deities and relying on them for protection. Because everything in nature has an owner, when you take something, you view it as a gift. One way to repay the benevolence of the spirits is through ritual offerings. In this view, oboo function as a shrine, where spirits dwell or gather. (Mongols believe that spirits inhabit high mountains or lonely hills but also mountain passes and road junctions.)

Initially, shamanist oboo were simple structures. In writing about early oboo, the nineteenth-century Buryat scholar Dorji Banzarov reported in *The Black Faith or Shamanism among the Mongols* that "a shaman usually announced that spirits who were patrons of a hill or a mountain selected this specific locality as their residence. Then, at a designated place, people erected obo, a small pile of stones and dirt, and performed proper rituals in honor of a territorial spirit." With the introduction of Buddhism in the seventeenth century, however, oboo construction became more complex.

* Variant forms include *obo*, *vebo*, and *owoo*. *Oboo* comes from the Mongolian written form *oboga*, which means "cairn."

122

They still needed to use stone, because it symbolized longevity and embodied strength, but now builders had to incorporate four colored minerals, one for each of the cardinal directions. They needed to embellish the sides with representations of numerous animals, such as tiger, elephant, and yak, and this didn't include the twelve zodiacal animals, the seven jewels, and the five sensuous qualities, which adorned the lower levels of the oboo. Finally, on the bottom the builder placed sacrificial cakes, amulets, and talismans that warded off the evils from birthmarks.

Territorial and community divisions also dictated how and where you worshipped an oboo. A former territorial region known as a banner might have one central oboo, held sacred by all of the inhabitants. Nonlocal people were usually not permitted to worship at such oboo because local deities derive pleasure from local worshippers. Families also had their own oboo, known as *otog ogoviin oboo*, or "patrilineal oboo," which could be worshipped for generations. At passes or dangerous spots in the road, travelers could make offerings to oboo. They would normally leave a stone and walk around the oboo three times.

Mongolian oboo scholar Ganzorig Davaa-Ochir includes a prayer to one such oboo:

Ovoonii ikh ni tand	A lot of cairns (are) for you
Olznii ikh ni manid	A lot of gains (are) for me
Süriin ikh ni tand	A lot of the splendor is for you
Süldenii ikh ni manid	A lot of the grandeur is for me
Öndöriin ikh ni tand	A lot of the heights are for you
Ölziin ikh ni manid	A lot of the auspiciousness is for me

Not all oboo had a religious significance. In areas with no prominent feature such as a mountain or river, oboo served as boundary markers. They also identified dangerous spots or safe routes to travel and, if lined up like a cross, indicated direction.

Some of the greatest variation centers on how many oboo to erect at a single location. Thirteen is the most common, though sources cite 1, 3, 5, 7, 9, 19, 21, and 108. The custom of building thirteen comes from the Buddhist tradition: a main oboo represents Mount Sumeru, the center of the Buddhist universe, and twelve corresponds to smaller continents of the cosmology. But this optimal number may also derive from Genghis Khan and the thirteen war summits he held, each of which involved erecting an oboo. As ethnologists Ujiyediin Chuluu and Kevin Stuart noted in "Rethinking the Mongol Oboo," "One hardly knows what a certain number of oboo may mean."

What makes oboo different from many other cairns around the world is animal sacrifice. In shamanist tradition, offerings of sheep, yak, camel, bull, oxen, or horse—sometimes only specific parts, such as the head and shoulder blades—were placed in front of the oboo. These are known as *bayasgakhiin takhil*, or "delighting offerings," with different deities preferring different animal sacrifices. Historian Charles Bawden quoted one Buddhist leader, however, who condemned such sacrifices, noting that "the slaughter of innocent beasts and the use of their flesh...[is] an offering only in error." Instead, "virtuous and glorious" Buddhist offerings included cakes, fruit, soup, milk, liquor, buttered bread, and weapons.

Whether they sacrificed an animal or offered an inanimate object, worshippers practiced their ritual once or twice a year, most often in summer and autumn, times when people, animals, and deities are most active. The offerings honored a local god, who had been invited by a shaman or lama to inhabit the oboo. In some cases, the protective spirit, or *onggod*, was embodied by a small figurine made of felt, silk, cloth, skin, leather, or wood and then buried under the cairn. Some such figurines have been passed down from ancestor to ancestor.

Venerated for hundreds of years, oboo suffered during Communist rule. From the 1930s to 1989, it was illegal to worship oboo. Many of the ancient rituals have returned since the breakup of the Soviet Union, but modern Mongols' perception and use of oboo have also changed. They have erected oboo to honor poets, politicians, and writers, as well as to express national identity and protect land from developers. As the world changes, so do oboo; it is a fundamental part of the tradition and why people continue to worship them.

Honoring Henry

Henry David Thoreau and I might have had a few spats. Despite his apparent fondness for all things natural, he did not like building stone. In *Walden* he wrote, "To what end, pray, is so much stone hammered. . . . Nations are possessed with an insane ambition to perpetuate the memory of themselves by the amount of hammered stone they leave. . . . I love better to see stones in place." We might, however, have agreed on cairns. They are not stones left in place, but at least they are not stones altered by man or nation.

One of the things I like best about cairns is that people make them from found rocks and not from rocks cut, chiseled, or sawn for that purpose. Stones used in cairns invariably reflect the nature of the stone —where and how it formed and where and how it weathered—and not the nature of a person. In that way, I like to think that cairns honor Thoreau's preference for simple and honest architecture.

How splendid then that a specific cairn is "our oldest monument to Thoreau," in the words of James Dawson and his superbly researched "History of the Cairn." This particular cairn rises near where Thoreau's original house stood at Walden Pond. It has been a central memorial to him since a lady from Dubuque, Iowa, placed the first stone in 1872.

Thoreau had died ten years earlier and had not lived at Walden Pond since 1847, following his twenty-six-month-long experiment "to anticipate, not the sunrise and the dawn merely, but, if possible, Nature herself!" Thoreau's 10-by-15-foot house had long been gone too. In 1849, it had been moved across Concord. The new owners stored corn in it. They would later demolish it and use the wood for construction on their farm.

By the early 1870s, Thoreau's fame had led to a regular stream of pilgrims seeking out Walden. They found little physical evidence to mark Thoreau's life until July 1872, when Bronson Alcott, father of Louisa May, visited with his Iowa friend Mary Newbury Adams and showed her where the small cabin had once stood. Noting that it was pity that nothing marked the spot, Adams suggested building a cairn and "then let[ting] everyone who loved Thoreau add a stone." Alcott, a lifelong friend of Thoreau's, agreed and added a stone to the one left by Adams. He noted in his journal entry for July 12–13, "Henry's fame is sure to brighten with years, and this spot be visited by admiring readers of his works." Little did Alcott know how prophetic his words would be.

By 1879, the date of the oldest drawing of the cairn, it was thigh high. Ralph Waldo Emerson had added a stone. A group of Unitarians had too, as had more than thirty-six spiritualists, who left inscribed rocks as part of a hundred-person-strong quest to honor Thoreau. Other stones would soon be left by Walt Whitman, John Burroughs, and John Muir.

Piling up stones to honor a person or event extends back deep into human history. We find such memorial cairns from Bronze Age Europe, across the Americas, and high on Himalayan peaks. Most are like Henry's, built up stone by stone by admirers, family, or friends. The use of rock to honor our fallen ones must be part of the essential human DNA. It's not just that we recognize the permanence of stone, but also that we realize the oneness of our planet, how we are all part of the same big rock, and that when we place a stone on a ceremonial cairn we are establishing an intrinsic connection with that person and that place. Or as Thoreau put it, "The whole earth is but a hero's cairn."

For 103 years, the cairn at Walden Pond continued to attract Thoreau's admirers. Part of it was moved in 1945, when archaeologist Roland Wells Robbins rediscovered the original site of Thoreau's cabin under part of the cairn, but otherwise the stone pile had simply grown larger and become more famous. Then in 1975, pilgrims, including forty Japanese students, each carrying a stone from home, arrived to discover that the cairn was no more.

The Massachusetts Department of Environmental Management, which oversaw what had by then become Walden Pond State Reservation, had determined that the cairn's location precipitated vandalism, in part because few understood the pile's significance. They considered adding an interpretive sign but deemed it would clutter the area, so they initially put the stones in "safe storage" and later moved them behind the reservation's headquarters, clear on the other side of Walden Pond from Thoreau's cabin site.

You can imagine the response. "Outrageous!! Thoreau would have been turning over in one of his two grave sites under one of his three tombstones if he knew," wrote James Dawson in *The Thoreau Society Bulletin*. The Thoreau Society sent letters, passed a resolution condemning the action, and met with officials. When the state rebuilt the cairn back in its rightful location, the bulletin's editor responded in the Summer 1978 issue, THE CAIRN IS BACK!!!!

Adding stones to the cairn is as popular as ever.* The Walden Woods Project, a nonprofit organization committed to preserving Thoreau's legacy, even leads tours where they encourage people to "leave behind a stone from your hometown at the Cairn." But controversy still lingers.

"I saw some graffiti yesterday that nearly took my breath away. Gravity-defying stacks of stone are desecrating the memorial cairn that marks the site of Henry David Thoreau's house at Walden Pond," wrote Robert Thorson in the September 20, 2007, *Hartford Courant*. He contends that Thoreau would not have approved of either the stacks' New Age spirituality or of the phallus-like towers, noting a passage in *Walden*: "One piece of good sense would be more memorable than a monument as high as the moon."

I agree with Thorson. Leaving a single stone, particularly one brought from one's home, seems appropriate, such a primal gesture in honor of the man who wrote "Simplicity. Simplicity. Simplicity!" It is anonymous, does not draw attention to oneself, and does not displace another's homage to Thoreau. At least these high-stone-stackers didn't carry off any of the sacred rocks, which apparently some people thought was the purpose of the cairn: Thoreau scholar James Dawson once overheard a visitor say to another, "Oh, it is all right to take a stone, that's why they pile them up here—for tourists to take."

Beinakerlingar: The Old Crones of Iceland

Earlier I joked that certain insect mating rituals performed near cairns might not be appropriate for children to see. Again, I am returning to sex and cairns, two subjects that might not seem connected, but they are, or at least were, in Iceland.

---

* In 1993, chunks of the Berlin Wall went into the cairn.

For example, consider this poem found in a cairn on the peninsula north of Reykjavík:

Þott aldrei fái átt við mig	Though he'd never get his way with me
ömurlegri þrjótur	The miserable man
skal ég aumkvast yfir þig —	I will take pity on you —
ef þú verður fljótur	If you are quick.

Starting in the late 1700s and maybe earlier, a tradition began in Iceland of leaving writings in the leg bone of an animal, such as a cow or sheep, and embedding that bone in a cairn. Initially, the cairn served as post office, or message board, with people alerting others to accidents, weather, natural hazards, or missing animals. Later, it became a game to leave a riddle or poem. If, say, a poet knew that someone was coming along, say, his wife, he might write a poem and tuck it into the cairn asking his wife not to spoil the relationship he had with the cairn. Over time the poems became a bit more bawdy, with the cairn taking on a more "doubtful character."

Others trace the origin of the cairn poems' sexual nature deeper into history, from more heathen times and worship of Freya, the goddess of beauty and love. Part of the ceremonies honoring Freya involved animal sacrifices, supplemented by maybe a few sexual liberties between worshipers. After the arrival of Christianity, the leaders frowned on such bacchanalian rituals. Leaving sexually suggestive poems in cairns was the last vestige of the good times.

Icelanders refer to cairns with such messages as *beinakerlingar*, from the singular *beinakerling*, a term of uncertain definition. (*Varða* is the Icelandic word for "cairn.") Folklorists define beinakerling most often as "bone crone," indicating that such cairns had taken on the personas of old women. Other definitions might be "bone cairn" or "female bone troll." *Beina* is usually translated as "bone" and *kerling* as "woman" or "old crone," though an Icelander I spoke with said that *kerling* is sort of the equivalent of "my old lady." It's not necessarily a nice term for a woman, nor is it that bad.*

---

* Off Drangey Island on the north coast of Iceland there is a couple-hundred-foot-tall sea stack known as Kerling. Legend holds that it is a female troll, turned to stone after getting caught out in the sun.

Just a few beinakerling poems have survived to modern times. One poem from the nineteenth century, left in a stone pile on a moss-covered basalt flow on the south end of Iceland, says, "May all be welcomed / that want to have me / I can't be satisfied / Alone on the mountain." Another, from the 1760s, was penned by a priest who worked for a senator. He placed the poem in a beinakerling on the road to the Alþingi, the national assembly. "If you, sir, want to grace my old age, / and find me alone in secret / then send away the lads."

One of my favorites comes from the eighteenth century and was left for a bishop:

> My good Sir from Hólar
> you are quite busy
> sleeping with me in the bed
> as it should be
>
> I have lost both my power and strength
> rejected many friends,
> I have waited all night long
> for the bishop.

Clearly the old women of the cairns had some fun.

No one knows how many beinakerlingar dotted Iceland, though there may have been as few as ten important ones. One of the more famous, at Sprengisandur, a desolate basalt plain in the middle of Iceland, consisted of a single large cairn surrounded by twenty-four smaller daughter cairns. A pair of beinakerlingar on the peninsula south of Reykjavík was named Kris and Herdis after two witches who had fought and killed each other. On a dirt road north from Þingvellir through the Kaldidalur (Cold Valley) is probably the most visited modern beinakerling, a massive pile, 10 feet tall by 25 feet wide at the base. Few if any visitors realize, however, that the Kaldidalur cairn has such a history of ribald poetry; I could find no guidebook that mentioned its past.

In a thoughtful consideration of beinakerlingar, medievalist scholars Marijane Osborn and Gillian Overing analyze how the cairns relate to the place of women, particularly older ones, in the wilderness. To Osborn and Overing, beinakerlingar serve as a twofold icon, signaling on the one hand old women finding a social function as message bearers and on the other young women at risk of losing their identity when alone in the wilderness. By endowing the cairn with story and purpose, the old woman of the beinakerling crosses boundaries and challenges our categories. Overing writes, "The capacity to acknowledge, engage—even celebrate—paradox is for me peculiarly Icelandic . . . where lines remain permanently—and wonderfully—crossed."

Tlingit Nests: Flood Refuges of the North

Not all floods are natural. The Tlingit people of southeastern Alaska have a legend that the ever inquisitive Raven wished to see what lay under the ocean. He accomplished this by asking the woman who controlled the tides to raise the water such that he could journey under it. She did so in a very slow manner that allowed the people to load their belongings into canoes and float up with the rising water. Being in southeastern Alaska, the Tlingit found refuge on the high peaks that surrounded their now submerged homes.

Bears and other wild animals also prowled the mountains. When they saw the people they swam toward them. In order to protect themselves, the people built rock walls, or "nests," and tied their canoes inside. Those who had dogs relied on them to help drive away the bears. Those who didn't perished.

In referring to the nests, ethnographer George Emmons, who studied the Tlingit in the late 1800s, wrote, "More baffling than petroglyphs and stone carvings are cairns of piled stones to be found on the mountains well above timberline." He noted at least ten cairns on the tops of mountains. They were three to four feet high and either pyramidal, round, or shaped like a J. They were far away from normal travel routes, did not mark boundaries, and did not appear to have any connection with the Russian occupation of the region.

When archaeologist Frederica de Laguna visited the Tlingit in 1949 and 1950, she heard similar stories involving Raven and the Flood. She also met a man who, as a young child, had visited some of the nests on Table Mountain, a peak on the south end of Admiralty Island. He told De Laguna that "when he had 'fooled around' on top of the mountains, it rained, and the old people knew that he had been naughty."

In the summer of 1995, Smithsonian archaeologist Aron Crowell and others spent six weeks investigating cultural remains in Glacier Bay National Park. His team located twenty-three cairns on three mountain-tops near Dundas Bay. They could not determine an exact age, but thick mats of lichens and mosses covering most of the cairns suggested a great antiquity. None of the cairns were conspicuous enough to mark boundaries or to serve as game drives. Nor did any contain a hollow interior indicative of a meat cache or fox trap.

Crowell's team concluded the Tlingit had built the cairns to commemorate the flood story. Their research also suggested that the story of Raven and the Flood may reflect actual events. During the Little Ice Age (1600s–1800s) and Neoglacial period (4,700–2,500 years ago), sea level fluctuated by as much as thirteen feet, leading to inundation of lowland communities.

Work by cultural anthropologists has shown that many Tlingit place names reflect changes in both sea level and in glacial advance and retreat. Crowell told me about *L'éiw Noowú* (Sandbar Fort), so named during a high-water periods when the fort could only be reached via a narrow raised sandbar. In contrast, *Xákwnoowú* (Dry Fort) refers to the same fort at a time of lower water, when it was first established and after the Little Ice Age. Another well-known place name, *Sit' Eeti Gheeyi* (The Bay in Place of the Glacier), refers to Glacier Bay and how the Muir Glacier has retreated since its greatest advance around 1775.

Few geographic names in Western culture reflect such a deep connection to the land. (Unless you count the irony of subdivisions named for what the development has eradicated: say, an Eagle Acres or Cougar Estates.) Western explorers generally named places for themselves, their friends, or their patrons. They did so in part to show ownership, but also because they had little knowledge or understanding of the history of the place. Perhaps we should establish a rule: if you think you need to name a place, you should have to live there long enough to develop true and real stories.

The truths that lie at the heart of the Tlingit Raven and Flood story illustrate what could be called the deep time of humanity. Deep time for geology involves millions of years. Deep time for humans involves hundreds and thousands of years. In those thousands of years may be profound lessons we can learn if we take the time to observe and ask questions and are willing to keep stories alive.

Carn Cafall

Did you know that King Arthur had a dog? He had several, but only one name has made it down to the present. That dog was Cafall, or Cabal, depending on which source you read. Apparently he was a rather large beast; one author has traced the origin of the name to the Welsh for "horse." We know this dog's name because he aided Arthur on a hunt, which was recorded at the beginning of the ninth century in the Welsh book *Historia Brittonum*.

According to the legend, Arthur, Cafall, and an army of soldiers and knights were hunting the notoriously nasty and mean-spirited boar Twrch Trwyth. (He had reason to be upset, as he was a former king now transformed into a boar.) Beginning in Cornwall, the hunters followed Twrch Trwyth to Ireland, then to Wales, back to Ireland, and again to Wales before finally driving the boar into the sea off Cornwall. The *Historia Brittonum* tells us that while chasing the formidable pig through central Wales near the town of Builth, Cafall "impressed [a] stone with the print of his foot." To honor this amazing geologic feat, Arthur built a cairn beneath the imprinted stone. Then the story becomes mystical, notes the author of the *Historia*: "Men come and take the stone in their hands for the space of a day and a night, and on the morrow it is found upon the stone pile."*

---

* This is not the only cairn with a reappearing stone. At Cape St. Vincent, the southernmost point in Portugal, were cairns known as *moledros*. If someone took a stone from a moledro, it would magically show up again the next day, brought back by the legendary King Sebastian, who was also supposed to return and lead Portugal at its darkest hour. Others held that if someone took a stone from the moledro and placed it under their pillow, a soldier would appear, only to disappear again by turning to a stone in the cairn.

Carn Cafall, as the pile of stone became known, was quite large. In 1841, Reverend Thomas Price led an expedition to find the cairn and corroborate the story. He found a cairn at least 150 feet in circumference. Atop it was a stone about two feet long by a foot wide bearing an oval dimple about the size of a potato. "Without any great strain of imagination," Price wrote, it could "be thought to resemble the print of a dog's foot." Although the indentation lacked any marks indicating toes or claws, one could suppose that a millennium of weather had removed these features.

I have a bit of trouble with this legend. As someone who considers himself fairly well educated about geologic processes, I find it hard to believe that Cafall, despite his great size, could have left his footprint in stone. Fossilized tracks and trackways certainly dot the geologic landscape, but in these situations the animals had generally left a mark in mud, which later turned to stone over a period of thousands to millions of years.

Whether the stone always returns to the cairn is another matter. I am not knowledgeable about such things. Nor did the phenomenon appear to bother the good Reverend Price, as he fails to mention any doubts about it. He does, though, question geologists. Alongside a drawing of Cafall's track, which does look like a couple-inch-deep hole in a rock, he wrote, "As the stone is a species of conglomerate, it is possible that some unimaginative geologist may persist in maintaining that this foot-print is nothing more than the cavity left by the removal of a rounded pebble, which was once imbedded in the stone; such an opinion scarcely requires a remark."

Of Darwin and Worms

Few, if any, people know that Charles Darwin wrote about cairns. In fact, I don't think he even knew that he wrote about them. Of course, this misunderstanding could arise because he didn't actually use the term *cairn*. Instead, he wrote about "little heaps of stones...[that] may frequently be seen on gravel-walks." As Darwin usually did, he wrote insightfully and based on his personal experience. In this case, the cairns rose in the yard at Down House, his home from 1842 till his death in 1882.

Darwin wrote about his study of cairns in his final book, *The Formation of Vegetable Moulds through the Action of Worms*, published just six months before he died. In the second chapter, on the habits of worms, Darwin noted that worms plugged up the mouths of their burrows with a mound of debris gathered from around the hole. Organic material, such as leaves, feathers, and tufts of wool, was most common, but a worm resorted to stones when they were available. (Some purists may question if these accumulations should be called a cairn, but Darwin himself referred to them as "heaps of smooth rounded pebbles," which I think qualifies.)

Others had noted this phenomenon too. A woman known as "I. W." had written to *The Gardeners' Chronicle and Agricultural Gazette* in March 1868. I. W. had removed several of the stone heaps from around burrow entrances, leaving a clearing of some inches. After two nights, she wrote, the earthworm burrows had "eight or nine small stones over them; after four nights one had about 30, another 24 stones." One worm had pulled a two-ounce-stone back to the heap by suction alone, using only its mouth. Curious as to the nature of the piles, I. W. wondered if readers could "throw any light on the subject."* (An average earthworm weighs about 0.1 ounce. If I could equal an earthworm's strength I would be able to drag a 3,000-pound walrus, not that the opportunity has arisen.) Darwin seconded I. W.'s observation of the worms' Herculean abilities, describing how they moved stones that had been firmly embedded in a gravel walkway.

More recently, Matt Canti, a geoarchaeologist with English Heritage, a government agency that protects historic places, has written about the stone piles in connection with how earthworms affect archaeological sites. Canti actually uses the term *cairn*, writing that a single worm builds each cairn, the biggest of which measure up to seven inches in diameter. In rich environments, there may be as many as one hundred cairns, or middens as some call them, per square yard. Some of these earthworm cairns have been found to last for four years. Although none have been found in the archaeological record, Canti notes that the worms' reworking of soils has had a significant effect on soils at archaeological sites.

---

* Darwin apparently knew this person, because he referred to I. W. as she in his book on earthworms.

Worms are not the only animals to move stones. Several species of birds are well known for this trait. The desert lark, a ground nester found in the Middle East, builds stone walls (about two inches high) in front of its nest, which ornithologist Yosef Orr described as a "pebble glacis," a type of defensive barrier found in medieval fortresses. In contrast, the rock wren of the American Southwest appears to be more friendly, constructing nests with stone driveways, one of which contained 728 pebbles ranging from one-half to two inches long.*

Most impressive, though, is the black wheatear, known in Spain as *pedrero*, the "stone quarrier" or "stonemason." During breeding season, a male will pick up an average of 277 stones and fly them back to the nest area. He deposits them in a pile, some of which contain up to four pounds of rock. The piles provide no benefit; the stones neither discourage predators, protect against weather, nor moderate temperatures. Instead, the females use the males' stone-toting facility to determine how much effort he will provide in raising their brood. I can just imagine her thinking, "Now, there is some good mating material."

Darwin could never figure out exactly why worms built their little heaps of stone. He questioned the idea that the stones prevented water from entering the burrow during rainstorms. Perhaps the heaps hid the burrow entrances from centipedes or checked the cold air from entering. Darwin leaned toward the latter view, though he also thought the cairns could serve all of these purposes.

Still considered to be a classic of natural history, Darwin's worm book initially sold faster than *On the Origin of Species*. Was it a coincidence that it mentioned cairns? I think not.

Two Cairns of Ice

Certainly one of the most heartbreaking and challenging cairns ever built was an ice cairn erected on January 18, 1912, at the South Pole. Having traveled eight hundred miles across Antarctica, Robert Falcon Scott and

---

* Early ornithologist Philo Smith hypothesized that this behavior might help the birds recognize their nest cavity from the multitude of holes found in cliff faces or that the walkway kept "the young birds from falling into crevices or getting their feet caught in the same." To this day no one knows the real reason.

his four remaining crew members knew that they had lost the race to the pole to Norwegian Roald Amundsen, but they still wanted to establish that they had obtained their goal. Scott wrote in his journal, "We built a cairn, put up our poor slighted Union Jack, and photographed ourselves—mighty cold work of it." One wonders how Scott and his men must have felt to know that their heroic effort was all in vain. Being stoic Brits, they never reveal their feelings in their journals.

Scott Memorial cairn

Amundsen and his team of four had reached the pole on December 14, 1911. One of them, Olav Bjaaland, wrote in his journal, "The excitement is great. Shall we see the English flag—God have mercy on us, I don't believe it." For the next three days, the Norwegians recorded regular observations of the sun to determine their exact location. "It is very difficult to arrive at a definitive result. But we can say with certainty that we are south of 89°59'," wrote Amundsen. A 1944 analysis of their data determined that they were very close, at 89°58'45" S, 71°36' E, a bit more than a mile from the pole.

Amundsen didn't build a cairn at the spot he determined to be the pole. He had built two small cairns earlier that Scott would pass. At the pole he left a tent, notes for Scott, a letter to the King of Norway (to prove Amundsen had been there), some equipment, and a plate with the name of the first five men to reach the South Pole. Flying above was the Norwegian flag and pennant from Amundsen's ship the *Fram*.

After Scott and his men finished their cairn, they turned north back to their base camp. They never made it; one died on February 17 and another on March 16. The surviving three died sometime around March 29, about eleven nautical miles from a large cache of food. Not found until November 12, they were left on the spot, buried under a large cairn of ice blocks.

In the intervening century, both Scott's cairn at the South Pole and the cairn that entombs him have moved. The first has traveled less, around two-thirds of a mile, placing it about 185 yards closer to the pole. It is estimated to be under about 56 feet of accumulated ice and snow. Located on the Ross Ice Shelf, the burial cairn has moved around forty miles and has been buried by 53 feet of snow. A report in December 2010 predicted that it should reach the edge of the ice sheet in the year 2250, under another 275 feet of ice. At that point, Scott and his men will most likely end up in a iceberg, floating farther away from the pole.

The Mile-High Cairn at the End of the Appalachian Trail

Tens of thousands of people reach the summit of Katahdin each year. For several hundred of them, the mountaintop in central Maine is the end point of their 2,180-mile-long trek of the Appalachian Trail. "For these thru-hikers, reaching the peak and touching the summit cairn is one of the great goals of their months-long trail experience, and likely one of the highlights of their life," writes John Neff in *Katahdin: An Historic Journey.*

In addition to being a long-sought goal, Katahdin's summit cairn has obtained a secondary bit of notoriety. It is generally said to be 13 feet high, which pushes the top of Katahdin to exactly 5,280 feet, or one mile above sea level. No one knows when the cairn obtained that noteworthy stature but it was not until at least 1927, when surveyor Floyd Neary determined that the peak's elevation was 5,267 feet. Until Neary came along, people's estimates of Kathadin's height bounced around from 5,150 to 5,623 feet.*

Surveyor Charles Turner Jr. and six men are the first people known to have climbed Catardin, as Turner labeled it. (The Native people of the area believed that a wrathful god known as Pamola took vengeance on those who tried to climb the mountain, so they never went up it.) The team reached the summit at 5:00 PM on August 13, 1804. They did not build a cairn. Instead they cut their initials into a sheet of lead and left it and a bottle of rum on the summit. It is not clear how good a surveyor Turner was, as he estimated the mountain's height to be 13,000 feet.

Sporadic visitors attempted to climb Katahdin over the next several decades. These include Maine's first state geologist (1837), Charles Thomas Jackson, who thought that Noah's flood had deposited boulders on the summit, and Henry David Thoreau (1846), who described "Ktaadn" as a "cloud-factory." A year later, the expedition of Maine's state botanist, Aaron Young Jr., made the first report of a summit cairn. Naturalist George Thurber wrote that "the declining day warned us to hasten our departure, and each one adding a stone to the rough monument there, we all joined in singing Old Hundred." Famous for his keen

---

* Whether the summit cairn is exactly 13 feet tall is subject to some debate. There is no official measurement of it. John Neff told me that "in regard to the 13-foot-cairn, I agree that the idea might have been achieved back when the elevation was settled, but I have never had the impression that was something that was kept up for too many years." Even if it is an apocryphal story, I suspect it won't fade away.

observations, Thoreau may not have mentioned or seen the cairn because he didn't reach the summit.

By 1853, writes John Neff, there was "a considerable rock cairn supporting a bottle containing birch bark pieces inscribed with the names and dates of other climbers." This large cairn could be the origin of an early name, Monument Peak, for the high point on Katahdin. The Maine legislature changed that name to Baxter Peak in 1931, in honor of Maine governor Percival Baxter (1921–24), who donated the lands surrounding Katahdin to the state. Katahdin means "greatest mountain," so it is redundant to say Mount Katahdin.

Photographs from the turn of the twentieth century show that the one cairn had multiplied to two, each about five feet high. No one knows why there were two or when the second one disappeared, but just one cairn has been on the summit since the 1930s. Historically, the Appalachian Mountain Club maintained a summit register, kept in a metal cylinder in the cairn. Replaced by a trailhead register, it appears to have been removed in 1960s.

With the completion of the Appalachian Trail in 1937, Katahdin became a point of pilgrimage. More than eleven thousand people, whether thru-hiking or section-hiking, have completed the trail. I suspect that most of them would agree with John Neff's sentiments.

Inuksuk

Like any good marketing entity, the Vancouver Organizing Committee for the 2010 Olympic and Paralympic Winter Games (VANOC) sought to brand itself. Paramount to their plan was a contest to design a logo for the Olympics. The winning designer would receive twenty-five thousand dollars, two tickets to the opening ceremonies, and a ton of press coverage. More than sixteen hundred entries poured into VANOC's offices.

VANOC officials presented the winning design on April 23, 2005, at an elaborate ceremony attended by nine thousand people and hordes of journalists. Assembled on center stage and then hoisted high above, the design featured a square green head, with a slightly ajar mouth, one red leg, one yellow leg, and a light-blue torso topped by a long horizontal rectangle of dark blue. The colors represented the natural attributes of Canada: green for forests, ocean blue for the coasts, alpine-glow yellow for sunset and sunrise, glacial blue for the mountains, and the red of the maple leaf. Designed by Elena Rivera MacGregor and Gonzalo Alatorre, the logo even had a name, Ilanaaq, or "friend" in the Inuit language.

"This smiling, confident, common figure reflects our sheer joy for winter sport and draws its strength from the true spirit of teamwork," said John Furlong, VANOC's CEO. He told the *Vancouver Sun* that the chunky figure was an *inuksuk*, an Inuit symbol made of stone and used to guide Inuit travelers. "It helps remind us to be true to our hearts, to give, to be wise, to have courage and, if we fail, it inspires us to get back up and to never ever quit."

MacGregor said that she had been inspired by a granite inuksuk she had seen in a park in Vancouver. Nunavat artist Alvin Kanak made the piece for the 1986 Vancouver World's Fair. After the fair, the eighteen-foot-high inuksuk had been moved to a permanent location overlooking English Bay. "Ilanaaq sends a message that Canada is welcoming the world to the 2010 Olympic games," MacGregor said in a promotional video.

Not everyone, however, took to Ilanaaq as Furlong did. "It doesn't look like a smile," graphic designer Ken Rodmell told a *Globe and Mail* reporter. "It's menacing, like he's some slightly crazed giant, or a monster from a horror movie. It has no neck. The head is square. It's flat on top. This is Frankenstein." Others thought it resembled Gumby with a rocket launcher. An editorial in Victoria's *Times-Colonist* opined that Furlong's high ideals seemed a "pretty big assignment for a pile of rocks. . . . At least they could have put the thing on skis."

Some might say that this was typical grousing about a new, odd-looking symbol. After all, Ilanaaq was supposed to represent Canadians to the world, which meant that the long-beloved maple leaf was out and a pile of rocks with a green Pac Manesque head was in.

Surprisingly, the most vociferous opposition to Ilanaaq came from the coastal aboriginal community. "It's kind of like a poke in the eye to First Nations people and First Nations artists," said Chief Edward John of the

First Nations Summit, a coalition of British Columbia's Native peoples. He told the *Globe and Mail* that he mainly objected to how inuksuk represented the northern part of Canada, completely omitting the influence of coastal groups and coastal symbols, such as the totem pole.

Paul Okalik, premier of the northern Canada territory of Nunavat, liked the inuksuk symbol, pointing out that no maple trees grow in the Arctic terrain that comprises much of the Inuit landscape. "Iconic Canadian images are often foreign to us. Ilanaaq changed that. For Ilanaaq to welcome visitors to Canada and inuksuit [plural of inuksuk] to remind them of their visit, Inuit are very proud," he told the *Globe and Mail*. The Inuit would also gain financially, as twelve hundred Native artists would spend two years carving thousands of six-inch- and ten-inch-high inuksuit to sell at the games in Vancouver. The smaller figure would cost $65 and the larger one $200.

Whether or not Ilanaaq was an appropriate or even a good-looking symbol for the Vancouver games became marginalized by bigger concerns, in particular either the selling of Ilanaaq as a physical object or for use in corporate marketing. As Elena Rivera MacGregor bluntly said to the *Globe and Mail*, "[The] logo had to fit as much in a Visa card as it did in a stadium or in the middle of an ice rink." By the time the games rolled around, Ilanaaq was everywhere—gracing coins, key chains, water bottles, hockey sticks, lapel pins, T-shirts—and the inuksuk had become a new symbol of Canada.

There was only one problem: Ilanaaq was not an inuksuk, according to Norman Hallendy, a Canadian public servant who has studied inuksuk since the 1960s. He noted that the proper Inuit term for Ilanaaq is *innunguag* (plural *innunguait*), or "in the likeness of a human," whereas *inuksuk* translates to "that which acts in the capacity of a human."

Hallendy has written extensively about inuksuit. His best-known publications are *Tukiliit: The Stone People Who Live in the Wind* and *Inuksuit: Silent Messengers of the Arctic*. The second book in particular tells of Hallendy's long-term journey to understand the people who build inuksuit and the landscape and traditions where they live. It is poetic, mystical, and deeply reverential.

INUKSUIT BY ANOTHER NAME

There is an old trope that the Eskimo have dozens of words for snow. Discounting the misuse of the term *Eskimo*, this cliché is not true. There are, however, dozens of ways to describe the inuksuit of the Inuit. In his thoughtful book, *Inuksuit: Silent Messengers of the Arctic*, Norman Hallendy compiles a list of more than fifty-five variations, which I have abbreviated here.

GENERAL TYPES OF INUKSUIT

inuksuapik • the most beautiful kind of inuksuk

inuksuk quviasunnirmik • an inuksuk that expresses joy, happiness

inuksullariunngittuqinuksutuinnaq • an unimportant inuksuk

inuksutuqaq • an old inuksuk

sakamaktaq • a great inuksuk demonstrating the strength of its builder

INUKSUIT RELATED TO HUNTING

inuksuk aiviqaijuqarnir • an inuksuk that signals a good place to hunt walrus

inuksuk iqaluqarniraijuq • an inuksuk of red and black stones that indicates a good place to fish

pirujaqarvik • an inuksuk that marks a meat cache

ulagutiit • inuksuit used to drive a caribou to shoot pits

usukjuaq • an inuksuk that indicates a rich spawning area and the direction in which to find it

INUKSUIT RELATED TO TRAVEL AND NAVIGATION

ikaarvik • an inuksuk that indicates a good place to cross a river

inuksuk nangiarautimik qaujimalitaq • an inuksuk that warns of danger

itiniqarniraijuq • an inuksuk that indicates the deep side of a river

turaaq • a simple inuksuk that is a flat stone pointing to the best (if not the quickest) route home

According to Hallendy's Inuit mentors, inuksuit date back to "the time of the earliest humans, those who prepared the land for our ancestors." Archaeologists date the earliest Canadian Arctic people to at least forty-five hundred years ago. Did they build inuksuit? We don't know, but it seems safe to think that they must have done so, considering the importance of marking one's way in this harsh region.

Hallendy lists five general types of inuksuit. At the most basic level are *nalunaikkutaq*, or "deconfusers," which may consist of just a single rock raised on end in order to remind someone of something. A "pointer," or *tikkuuti*, consists of a rock or several rocks aligned to indicate direction. *Inuksummarik* are another form of directional marker, made of a large pyramid of boulders and visible from a distance. The ones known as *niungvaliruluit* are shaped like a window and are used to create sight-lines to other inuksuit. There are also more private inuksuit that contain meanings or messages meant for a tight group, such as hunting party.

As in other cultures around the world, the Inuit put up stone structures for memorial purposes too. After a battle in 1940, the victors erected *inuksuit upigigaugialait* to honor the dead souls of the vanquished. More recently, these types of memorials have been built in Kandahar, Afghanistan, and at Juno Beach, the site of D-Day landings in Normandy, France.

Because they "act in the capacity of a human," inuksuit often play an important role in hunting. On Baffin Island, Hallendy came across an area with more than a hundred inuksuit, built in two sizes: the height of a standing hunter and the height of a seated figure. Hallendy's Inuit hunter friends told him that the inuksuit had been built to habituate geese to the presence of "hunters." When the real hunters returned, they would find it much easier to approach the geese. "Season after season the hunters captured and killed many birds," Hallendy wrote.

People have long used stone piles to fool animals during hunting. One common practice in areas with few trees has been to set up extended rows of cairns known as game drives. Some of the oldest well-documented game drives were built above timberline in Colorado's Rocky Mountains and date back more than nine thousand years to just after the end of the last Ice Age. Placed in order to direct animals, such as elk and bighorn, downwind to waiting hunters, the several hundred drives consisted of lines of cairns and low walls in a U or funnel shape. A distance of 6 to 12 feet separated the cairns, with walls stretching for more than 3,000 feet. Because the regional topography forced animals to follow predictable migration routes, early hunters could have used the same drives for generations.

Established much later, because the Laurentide Ice Sheet still covered the area and submerged it below sea level, game drives in the Arctic functioned in a similar way to ones in Colorado. They were a perfect place for inuksuit, often as simple as a propped-up long narrow slab. Many were adorned in order to create movement that scared caribou. In the northern Quebec territory of Nunavik, the people built *aulaqquit,* or "scarecrows," which bore dried, outstretched gull wings hanging on lines of sinew, while Baffin Islanders hung plants or caribou ribs and scapula.

The introduction of the horse led to the abandonment of the Colorado game drives in the 1700s. As the function of the rows of cairns faded from memory, bizarre explanations came up. My favorite is that Indians built them so that their ponies would have stepping stones to cross deep snow in spring. Similarly, the introduction of snowmobiles has reduced people's reliance on game drives in the Arctic, though one Canadian government report described how Inuit in the Northwest Territories built inuksuit drive lines in the late 1990s to divert caribou herds around a diamond mine.

Reading Hallendy's book, it is clear that his Inuit friends have an intimate relationship with the land. Their survival depends on observing subtle changes in all aspects of the natural world, such as topography; snow accumulation and melting; the speed, direction, and sound of water and wind movement; where and how plants grow and what they smell like; when animals migrate, shed feathers, fur, or antlers; and when animals rut, lay eggs, give birth, and build nests. For example, in *Arctic Dreams,* Barry Lopez writes about how, on a foggy day in summer, a traveler on shore-fast ice would stick to a route bounded by the calls of cliff-dwelling seabirds and surf sounds on the seaward edge of the ice. To live in the

Arctic requires paying attention to clues, no matter the form and often only learned from generations of ancestors doing the same thing.

Many visitors to the north have commented on the amazing accuracy with which Native people are able to render maps, some of which cover hundreds of square miles. Where the maps differ from those drawn with more sophisticated tools is that Native peoples emphasize places of importance by drawing them slightly out of proportion. They know the details of landscape, but they also know that their landscape could not be separated from their lives; you can't draw the land without revealing strands that connect place and people.

Understanding the place where you live and knowing its intimate topography means more than having the ability to move simply from place A to place B. It means knowing when to make that movement in order to do it safely or when to travel a different path because the planned route has obstacles not normally found there. It means knowing when and where animals will be available to hunt. It means knowing the stories of the land. And there is nothing wrong with relying on a little help from your friends in the form of an inuksuk.

ACKNOWLEDGMENTS

First and foremost I would like to thank Kate Rogers who suggested this idea to me. It has been a fun adventure. I would also like to thank Julie Van Pelt for her thoughtful and thorough copyediting.

Thanks also to Robert Anderson, Will Gadd, Glen Lathrop, Shannon Huffman Polson, Craig Romano, Matt Samet, John Sanford, and Linda Versage for sharing their cairn stories with me.

I appreciate all those who took time to answer my many questions either via email, in person, or over the phone. Any misinterpretation or incorrect use of the facts is entirely my fault. Thanks to: Richard Armstrong, Jette Arneborg, Keola Awong, Marc Baldwin, Dan Beck, Matt Becker, Arni Björnsson, Tom Bradwell, Stephen Briggs, Bob Brunswig, David Butler, Ryan Calsbeek, Matt Canti, Steve Cassells, Tom Chambers, Tom Clare, Alison Colwell, Pete Cranston, Aron Crowell, Tim Darvill, Carl Davis, Carolyn Dean, Roger del Moral, Oliver Dickinson, Ivan and Carol Doig, Jim Feathers, Becky Fullerton, Todd Gehman, Ross Goldingay, Tim Graham, Jack Haskel, Chris Hiemstra, Jean Hoekwater, Denver Holt, Raymond Huey, Charlie

ACKNOWLEDGMENTS

Jacobi, Stephen Jett, Ken Jones, Didi Kaplan, Bill Laprade, Tomas Lipps, Tanzhuo Liu, Joxe Mallea-Olaetxe, Dan McCarthy, Susan McGrath, Diane McIlmoyle, Hawk Methany, Mark Miller, Chris Mitchell, Anders Pape Møller, Pamela Moriarty, Damon Murdo, John Neff, Martin Norgate, Suzanne Oppenheimer, Marijane Osborn, Joel Pederson, Anthony Pettendrup, Paul Picha, Jon Pierson, Eric Pinder, Russell Potter, Patrick Rennie, Lynn Resler, Chris Robertson, Anna Rühl, Peter Schledermann, Lin Schwarzkopf, Andrew Shapland, Larry St. Clair, Rick Shine, Bill Smith, Margrét Solvadottir, Rupert Soskin, Per Storemyr, Mike Sweeney, Robert Thorson, Jon Titus, Ricardo Tomé, Philip Vogler, Katie Wales, Scott Wanek, Adam Watson, Jonathan Webb, Caroline Wilson, and Michele Zwartjes.

I owe a deep well of gratitude to my good pals in the Unspeakables, who were always willing to lend an ear and offer encouragement. I look forward to many more fine meals together.

And, of course, to my wife, Marjorie, who put up with yet another book about rocks. You are the best.

SOURCES

Barber, John. *The Excavation of a Stalled Cairn at the Point of Cott, Westray, Orkney.* Monograph 1. Scottish Trust for Archaeological Research, 1997.

Baughman O'Leary, Shirley. *Stone Johnnies: Vanishing Landmarks of the Lonely Buttes.* Belle Fourche, SD: Sand Creek Printing, 2005.

Bawden, C. R. "Two Mongol Texts Concerning Obo-Worship." *Oriens Extremus* 5, no. 1 (October 1958): 23–41.

Beattie, O. B. "Elevated Bone Lead Levels in a Crewman from the Last Arctic Expedition of Sir John Franklin." In *The Franklin Era in Canadian Arctic History: 1845–1859*, Archaeological Survey of Canada, Mercury Series No. 131, ed. P. D. Sutherland, 141–48. Ottawa: National Museum of Man, 1985.

Beck, Daniel D., and Randy D. Jennings. "Habitat Use by Gila Monsters: The Importance of Shelters." *Herpetological Monographs* 17 (2003): 111–29.

Benedict, James B. "Tundra Game Drives: An Arctic-Alpine Comparison." *Arctic, Antarctic, and Alpine Research* 37, no. 4 (2005): 425–34.

Beschel, Roland. "Dating Rock Surfaces by Lichen Growth and Its Applications to Glaciology and Physiography (Lichenometry)." In *Geology of the Arctic*, vol. 1, ed. G. O. Raasch, 1044–62. Toronto: University of Toronto Press, 1961.

Beston, Henry. *The Outermost House: A Year of Life on the Great Beach of Cape Cod*. New York: Henry Holt and Company, 1949.

Booth, B. D. McD. "Breeding of the Sooty Falcon in the Libyan Desert." *Ibis* 103A, no. 1 (January 1961): 129–30.

Bradley, Richard. *The Good Stones: A New Investigation of the Clava Cairns*. Edinburgh: Society of Antiquaries of Scotland, 2000.

Brooks, Geraldine. *Caleb's Crossing*. New York: Viking, 2011.

Burton, Richard. *Abeokuta and the Camaroons Mountains*. London: Tinsley Brothers, 1863.

Canti, M. G. "Earthworm Activity and Archaeological Stratigraphy: A Review of Products and Processes." *Journal of Archaeological Science* 30 (2003): 135–48.

Chartkoff, Joseph L. "A Rock Feature Complex from Northwestern California." *American Antiquity* 48, no. 4 (1983): 745–60.

Chittenden, Jacqueline. "The Master of Animals." *Hesperia: The Journal of the American School of Classical Studies at Athens* 16, no. 2 (April–June 1947): 89–114.

Chuluu, Ujiyediin, and Kevin Stuart. "Rethinking the Mongol Oboo." *Anthropos* 90 (1995): 544–54.

Darwin, Charles. *The Formaton of Vegetable Moulds through the Action of Worms, with Observations on Their Habits*. London: John Murray, 1881.

Davaa-Ochir, Ganzorig. "Oboo Worship: The Worship of Earth and Water Divinities in Mongolia." Master's thesis, University of Oslo, 2008.

Dawson, James. "A History of the Cairn." *Thoreau Society Bulletin*, no. 232 (Summer 2000).

Dean, Carolyn. "Rethinking Apacheta." *Nawpa Pacha* 28 (2006): 93–108.

de Laguna, Frederica. *The Story of a Tlingit Community: A Problem in the Relationship between Archeological, Ethnological, and Historical Methods.* Bureau of American Ethnology Bulletin 172. Washington, DC: US Government Printing Office, 1960.

Doig, Ivan. *Mountain Time.* New York: Scribner, 1999.

Eliade, Mircea. *Patterns in Comparative Religion.* New York: Sheed and Ward, 1998.

Emmons, George Thornton. *The Tlingit Indians.* Edited with additions by Frederica de Laguna and a biography by Jean Low. Seattle: University of Washington Press, 1991.

Epstein, Clare. *The Chalcolithic Culture of the Golan.* Jerusalem: Israel Antiquities Authority, 1998.

"The Fate of Franklin." *Athenæum*, October 28, 1854.

Fenwick, J. P. "A Note on Four Icelandic Cairns." *Man* 10 (1910): 22.

Fraser, David. *Land and Society in Neolithic Orkney.* Oxford, England, British Archaeological Reports 117, 1983.

Frazer, James. *The Golden Bough: A Study in Magic and Religion*, part VI, *The Scapegoat.* 3rd ed. London: Macmillan, 1913.

Goldsworthy, Andy. *Time.* New York: Harry N. Abrams, 2000.

Goulder, Dave. *Notes on Building a Cairn.* Crooksland, Cumbria: Dry Stone Walling Association of Great Britain, n.d.

Guthrie, A. B., Jr. "Who Was Peter Saddler." *Country Beautiful* (November 1961): 12–17.

Guthrie, W. K. C. *The Greeks and Their Gods.* London: Methuen, 1950.

Hallendy, Norman. *Inuksuit: Silent Messengers of the Arctic.* Vancouver, BC: Douglas & McIntyre Publishers, 2000.

------. *Tukiliit: The Stone People Who Live in the Wind.* Vancouver, BC: Douglas & McIntyre Publishers, 2009.

Headland, R. K. "Captain Scott's Last Camp, Ross Ice Shelf." *Polar Record* 47, no. 2 (2011): 270.

Hedges, John W. *Isbister: A Chambered Tomb in Orkney.* BAR British Series 115. Oxford: BAR, 1983.

Henshall, Audrey S., and J. N. Graham Ritchie. *The Chambered Cairns of the Central Highlands: An Inventory of the Structures and their Contents.* Edinburgh: Edinburgh University Press, 2001.

Homer. *Odyssey.* Translated by Stanley Lombardo. Indianapolis: Hackett, 2000.

Hopkins, Samuel. *Historical Memoirs, Relating to the Housatunnuk Indians.* Boston: S. Kneeland, 1753.

Huntford, Roland. *Race for the South Pole: The Expedition Diaries of Scott and Amundsen.* New York: Continuum, 2010.

Hyslop, John. *The Inka Road System.* Orlando: Academic Press, 1984.

Jett, Stephen C. "Cairn Trail Shrines of the Navajo, the Apache, and Puebloans, and of the Far North." In *Artifacts, Shrines, and Pueblos: Papers in Honor of Gordon Page,* ed. David T. Kirkpatrick and Meliha S. Duran. Albuquerque: Archaeological Society of New Mexico, 1994.

Kane, Elisha Kent. *The United States Grinnell Expedition in Search of Sir John Franklin.* New York: Harper and Brothers, 1854.

Kaplan, Didi. "The Enigma of the Establishment of *Quercus ithaburensis* Park Forest in Northern Israel: Co-Evolution of Wild Board and Men?" *Wildlife Biology* in Practice 2, no. 1 (2005): 95–107.

Livingstone, David. *Narrative of an Expedition to the Zambesi and Its Tributaries.* New York: Harper and Brothers, 1866.

Lumholtz, Carl. *Unknown Mexico.* Vol. 2. New York: Charles Scribner's Sons, 1902.

MacMillan, Donald B. *How Peary Reached the Pole: The Personal Story of His Assistant.* Montreal: McGill Queen's University Press, 2008.

Markham, Clement Robert. *Franklin's Footsteps*. London: Chapman and Hall, 1853.

Maynard, W. Barksdale. *Walden Pond: A History*. New York: Oxford University Press, 2004.

M'Clintock, Francis Leopold. *The Voyage of the "Fox" in the Arctic Seas*. London: John Murray, 1859.

M'Cormick, Robert. *Narrative of a Boat Expedition up the Wellington Channel*. London: George Edward Eyre and William Spottiswoode, 1854.

McCullough, Karen, and Peter Schledermann. "Mystery Cairns on Washington Irving Island." *Polar Record* 35 (1999): 289–98.

Miller, Mark E. "*An Ethnohistoric Perspective on Winter Sheep Camps in South Central Wyoming, 1880–1937*." Unpublished, 2011.

Mitchell, Christopher. *Lake District Natural History Walks*: Case Notes of Nature Detective. Wilmslow, Cheshire, England: Sigma Leisure, 2004.

Mongé, Alf. *A Guide to the Solution of Runic Cryptography*, vol. 5, *Solutions*. Landsverk Foundation, 1980.

Moss, Edward L. *Shores of the Polar Sea: A Narrative of the Arctic Expedition of 1875–6*. London: Marcus Ward and Co., 1878.

Murphy, David. *The Arctic Fox: Francis Leopold McClintock, Discoverer of the Fate of Franklin*. Toronto: Dundurn Press, 2004.

Nares, George S. *Narrative of a Voyage to the Polar Sea during 1875–76 in H.M. Ships Alert and Discovery*. London: Sampson Low, Marston, Searle and Rivington, 1878.

Neff, John. Katahdin: *An Historic Journey; Legends, Exploration, and Preservation of Maine's Highest Peak*. Boston: Appalachian Mountain Club Books, 2006.

Orheim, Olav. "The Present Location of the Tent That Roald Amundsen Left Behind at the South Pole in December 1911." *Polar Record* 47, no. 2 (2011): 268–70.

Orr, Yosef. "Temperature Measurements at the Nest of the Desert Lark (*Ammomanes deserti deserti*)." *The Condor* 72, no. 4. (October 1970): 476.

Osborn, Sherard. "Arctic Journal; or, Eighteen Months in the Polar Regions." In *Putnam's Semi-Monthly Library for Travelers and the Fireside* XIV (August 2, 1852).

Osborn, Marijane, and Gillian R. Overing. "Bone-Crones Have No Hearth: Some Women in the Medieval Wilderness." In *Textures of Place: Exploring Humanist Geographies*, ed. Paul C. Adams, Steven Hoelscher, and Karen E. Till. Minneapolis: University of Minnesota Press, 2001.

Price, A. Grenell, ed. *The Explorations of Captain James Cook in the Pacific as Told by Selections of His Own Journals, 1768–1779*. Mineola, NY: Dover, 1971.

Price, Thomas. *The Literary Remains of the Rev. Thomas Price*. Vol. 2. London: Llandovery, 1855.

Reilly, Stuart. "Processing the Dead in Neolithic Orkney." *Oxford Journal of Archaeology* 22, no. 2 (2003): 133–54.

Renfrew, Colin. *Investigations in Orkney. Reports of the Research Committee of the Society of Antiquaries of London* No. 38. London, 1979.

Report of the Committee Appointed by the Lords Commissioners of the Admiralty. London: George Edward Eyre and William Spottiswoode, 1852.

Ridgeway, Ann N., ed. *The Selected Letters of Robinson Jeffers, 1897–1962*. Baltimore: Johns Hopkins University Press, 1968.

Sharples, Niall, and Alison Sheridan, eds. *Vessels for the Ancestors: Essays on the Neolithic of Britain and Ireland in Honour of Audrey Henshall*. Edinburgh: Edinburgh University Press, 1992.

Smith, Philo W. "Nesting Habits of the Rock Wren." *The Condor* 6, no. 4 (July 1904): 109–10.

Smucker, Samuel M., ed. *Arctic Explorations and Discoveries during the Nineteenth Century.* New York: Miller, Orton and Co., 1857.

"Soup Can Reopens Mystery of Doomed Franklin Expedition." *Daily News* (McMaster University), December 15, 2009.

Stevenson, Matilda Coxe. "The Zuni Indians: Their Mythology, Esoteric Fraternities, and Ceremonies." In *Twenty-Third Annual Report of the Bureau of Ethnology.* Washington, DC, 1904.

Stringer, Peggy. "An Intimate Exploration of Rock Stacking as a Sacred Art Form Evoking the Numinous Experience." PhD diss., Pacifica Graduate Institute, 1999.

Sturm, Matthew, et. al. "Winter Biological Processes Could Help Convert Arctic Tundra to Shrubland." *BioScience* 55, no. 1 (January 2005): 17–26.

Thoreau, Henry David. *Journal Volume 2: 1842–1848.* Princeton, NJ: Princeton University Press, 1984.

Thorson, Robert. *Stone by Stone: The Magnificent History in New England's Stone Walls.* New York: Walker and Co., 2002.

Thurber, George. "Notes of an Excursion to Mount Katahdin." *Maine Naturalist* 6, no. 4. (December 1926): 134–51.

Tozzer, Alfred M. "Chronological Aspects of American Archaeology." *Massachusetts Historical Society Proceedings* 59 (1926): 283–92.

Van Valkenburgh, Richard F. "Sacred Places and Shrines of the Navajos: Part II." *Plateau* 13, no. 1 (July 1940): 6–9.

Yeend, W. E. "Winter Protalus Mounds: Brooks Range, Alaska." *Arctic and Alpine Research* 4, no. 1 (1972): 85–87.

INDEX

INDEX

ring cairns, 69, 71
ritualism, 85, 89
rock stacking, 107
rock varnish, 56–57
Rodmell, Ken, 140
Ross, James, 100
Rousay Island, 73–74

salt, 35
sandstone, 28-29, 35
Schledermann, Peter, 61
Scotland, 65–66, 71
Scott, Robert Falcon,
  135–37
Seattle, 23
sedimentary rock, 28–29
Sergeant, John, 77
Seton, Ernest Thompson,
  21
shapes, 34
sheepherder's
  monuments, 117, 119
Shine, Rick, 47
Siberia, 22
Sierra Nevada, 30
Sinervo, Barry, 47
sivivane, 11
slate, 31–32
snakes, 47
snow, 45
South Island, 97
South Ridge Trail, 15
South Ronaldsay Island,
  73–75
south-facing side, 45
Space Needle, 23
spreading center, 25
stacked stones, 104–13
stalled cairns, 69, 73
Stevenson, Matilda Coxe,
  83
Stewart, William, 65
stone Johnnies, 117, 119

stone stacking, 104–13
stone tools, 16
Tabor oak trees, 40–41
Tapsa Temple, 107
Tarahumara, 11
Terror, 91–92, 95–96,
  98, 101
thallus, 53
Thoreau, Henry David,
  53, 125–27, 138
Thorson, Robert, 37, 127
Tlingit nests, 130–32
tombolo, 95
tombs, 39, 71, 73
tor cairns, 69
Tor House, 112
trail marking, 10–11
trailside shrines, 77–89
transference of evil,
  81–82, 85–87
travertine, 28–29
tsé nindjihí, 11, 83–85
Tsountas, Christos, 120
tugong bula, 11
tumulus, 40
Turner, Charles Jr., 138

upfreezing, 36
upthrust rocks, 36
US Department of
  Agriculture, 20
US Geological Survey,
  109

Valrslethn, Oirvat, 62
Van Valkenburgh,
  Richard, 84
varda, 11
varnish microlaminations,
  57
Vikings, 74
volcanoes, 26–27

von Hagen, Victor
  Wolfgang, 79
Walden Pond, 125–26
water, 45
water-beaten rocks,
  33–34
Watkins, Alfred, 75
Watson, Adam, 66
weathering, 35–36
Webb, Jonathan, 47
wedge, 17
Westman Island, 26
Westray, 73
White Mountains, 30,
  32–33
wind, 44
worms, 133–35

Xanthoria elegans, 44, 52
Xanthoria parietina, 44

Yeend, Warren, 36
Yehudiya Forest Nature
  Preserve, 40–41
Yellowstone National
  Park, 26
Yi Gap Yong, 107
Yosemite National Park,
  109

zeroing, 58
Zulu, 11

ABOUT THE AUTHOR

David B. Williams is a natural history writer based in Seattle. He is the author of *Stories in Stone: Travels Through Urban Geology* and *The Seattle Street-Smart Naturalist: Field Notes from the City*. A regular contributor to *Earth* magazine and the *Seattle Times*, David is an avid hiker and biker and a former national park ranger in Utah and Boston.

OTHER TITLES YOU MIGHT ENJOY BY THE MOUNTAINEERS BOOKS

The Pacific Crest Trailside Reader: California
Rees Hughes and Corey Lee Lewis
Forty-nine stories of the Pacific Crest Trail in California,
written by real PCT hikers and aficionados.

The Pacific Crest Trailside Reader: Oregon and Washington
Rees Hughes and Corey Lewis
Forty-six short pieces of the "adventure, history, and legend"
of the Oregon and Washington segments of the PCT.

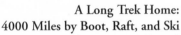

A Long Trek Home: 4000 Miles by Boot, Raft, and Ski
Erin McKittrick
A couple take a walk from Seattle, Washington
to Alaska's Aleutian Islands.

Steller's Island: Adventures of a Pioneer Naturalist in Alaska
Dean Littlepage
Georg Steller, who gave his name to the Steller's jay,
Steller's sea lion, and Steller's eider, brought the wilds of
Alaska to Europe in the mid-eighteenth century.

Faith of Cranes: Finding Hope and Family in Alaska
Hank Lentfer
"*Faith of Cranes* is a love song to the beauty and worth of the lives we
are able to lead in the world just as it is, troubled though it be."
—David James Duncan

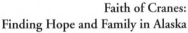

The Mountaineers Books has more than
500 outdoor, recreation, and adventure titles in print.
For details, visit
www.mountaineersbooks.org.